TESTIMONIALS

"**F**red Mitchell and Richard Dent have collaborated in presenting some fantastic insights into the world of professional football. The excitement, the travail, the hard work and dedication, the disappointments and the thrills are all captured in this wonderful work by these two fellows who have 'been there, done that'."

Marv Levy
Pro Football Hall of Fame Coach
Author

"**T**he Sack Man! A tower of power at right defensive end for the Chicago Bears. Richard Dent was an afterthought on Draft Day and yet became one of the most wicked pass rushers in NFL history.

"Dent tells his story – on and off the field – with the help of *Chicago Tribune* writer Fred Mitchell. This is truly a must read for Chicago Bears fans or anyone who appreciates pro football on the big-time level. Number 95 forced defensive coordinators to burn the midnight oil."

Chet Coppock
Chicago Sports Talk Radio

"**T**he first time I saw Richard Dent on the Bears practice field, I told people this guy was going to be something special. Richard became the real deal as a player, and he pulls no punches in his book as he reveals details of his life and Hall of Fame playing career as the Sack Man."

Dan Jiggetts, Chicago sportscaster and
former Bears offensive lineman

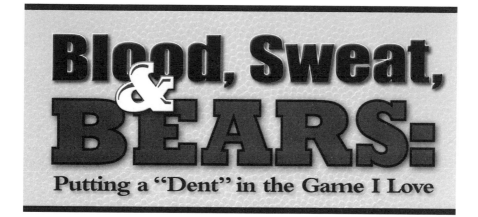

Blood, Sweat, & BEARS:
Putting a "Dent" in the Game I Love

RICHARD DENT
with Fred Mitchell

ASCEND BOOKS

www.ascendbooks.com

Requests for permission should be addressed to:
Ascend Books, LLC, Attn: Rights and Permission Department
12710 Pflumm Road, Suite 200, Olathe, KS 66062

All names, logos, and symbols that appear in this book are trademarks of their individual organizations and institutions. This notice is for the protection of trademark rights only, and in no way represents the approval or disapproval of the text of this book by those organizations or institutions.

10 9 8 7 6 5 4 3 2 1

ISBN: print book 978-0-9830619-8-4
ISBN: e-book 978-0-9830619-6-0
Library of Congress Cataloging-in-Publications Data Available Upon Request

Editor: Jeffrey Flanagan
Assistant Editor: Blake Hughes
Publication Coordinator: Christine Drummond
Sales and Marketing: Lenny Cohen
Dust Jacket and Book Design: Lynette Ubel

All photos courtesy of Richard Dent and Fred Mitchell unless otherwise indicated.

Use of the phrase The Shufflin Crew© courtesy of Red Label Music Publishing, Inc.

Every reasonable attempt has been made to determine the ownership of copyright. Please notify the publisher of any erroneous credits or omissions, and corrections will be made to subsequent editions/future printings.

The goal of the enitre staff of Ascend Book is to publish quality works. With that in mind, we are proud to offer this book to our readers. Please note however, that the story, the experiences and the words are those of the authors alone.

Printed in the United States of America

ASCEND BOOKS

www.ascendbooks.com

DEDICATION

This book is dedicated to
my mother, Mary Francis
Dent. I hope I made you smile;
I hope I made you proud.

From Richard

ACKNOWLEDGEMENTS

My life has been filled with plenty of ups and downs – exhilarating sports highlights and major accomplishments tempered by the kind of occasional humbling moments that all of us have to learn how to handle and endure.

Throughout it all, I stand tall and continue to strive to help others. My proud legacy is an ever-evolving story that will define my time here on earth.

I have so many people to thank when it comes to helping me tell my story through this book. That list includes Ascend Books Publisher Bob Snodgrass, Publications Coordinator Christine Drummond, Executive Editors Jeffrey Flanagan and Blake Hughes, Designer Lynette Ubel, and Publicity Director Bob Ibach.

I also would like to thank veteran sportswriter/author Fred Mitchell, who covered a great deal of my NFL playing career for the *Chicago Tribune* and helped me put my feelings and recollections into words.

My longtime personal assistant, Carol Freeman, was invaluable with her research work on this project. And I appreciate the photo resource information from Dan Yuska of the Chicago Bears and my friend, photographer Mike Kinyon and the statistical data gleaned from ProFootballHOF.com and the *Chicago Tribune*.

I also want to thank Dean Robert Murrell and his wife Dean Barbara Murrell from Tennessee State who kept me in school and took such good care of me.

To my former teammates and coaches at Murphy High School, Tennessee State and the NFL: Thanks for the memories.

Richard Dent

CONTENTS

Dedication VII

Acknowledgements IX

Chapter 1   Unfounded Suspicions 13

Chapter 2   My Love-Hate Relationship with Ditka 27

Chapter 3   Not Feeling the Love 41

Chapter 4   The Crazy Life of Being a Bear 65

Chapter 5   Flashback: A Tennessee State Tiger 75

Chapter 6   Sweetness 85

Chapter 7   Rushing the Quarterback 93

Chapter 8   Out of the Mouths of Bears 105

Chapter 9   Super Memories 145

Chapter 10   The Flip Side to Glory 153

Chapter 11   Losing a Friend 165

Chapter 12   Mutiny and the Bounty 181

Chapter 13   On My Way to Canton 195

Chapter 14   Oh, What a Season: The '85 Bears 217

Chapter 15   Unfinished Business 251

Appendix: My Career Stats 254

Unfounded Suspicions 1

One of the most disturbing experiences in my life occurred early in my NFL career when some members of the Chicago Bears organization questioned whether I was selling and using cocaine in the early 1980s.

It's bad enough when fans and media try to attack you. But when your own employer questions your character and integrity ... that really hurts me to the soul, even to this day.

I cannot overstate the pride I felt wearing that Bears uniform and representing the fans of Chicago. Not only did I feel that I was representing the fans, but I also was representing my family, the community where I grew up and the coaches I came to respect, from my childhood days through college. So there was no way I would choose to disrespect those people in my life by engaging in something patently illegal and so self-indulgent as selling drugs.

Prior to my days playing organized football, my life lacked the kind of structure, discipline and purpose necessary to put me on a path toward success. With each opportunity – from high school, college and the NFL – I had to demonstrate what kind of football player I could be. I gained confidence, poise, determination and pride. Those were my tickets to success.

No way I was going to screw this up.

Sadly, I had a lot of older brothers who had been involved in drugs and fighting and serious crimes. I had a first-hand look early in my life at how criminal and other mischievous behavior can really mess up your life and the lives of others who care about you.

I saw the pain first-hand that my brothers caused my mother. Nobody finished high school, nobody went to college, nobody fulfilled his dream. I was the first son to finish high school and the first son to go to college in my family. I was proud of that. The rest of the boys in my family just couldn't seem to find their way in life. Sure, they had individual talents, but they didn't get a chance to bloom and show the world all of the good they could have done through a worthwhile career. Such a shame, such a waste.

With such a big family, it was difficult for all of us to get the proper individual attention to make the right choices in life. I had to make the choices on my own, and I wanted to make somebody proud of me. That always has been a driving force. I wanted to be the one to make my parents proud. But it was a very, very rocky road.

It wasn't easy getting the direct attention of my parents, even after I made it as a college player at Tennessee State and as an impact player in the NFL. My parents didn't like to fly, so neither one of them ever came up to Chicago to see me play with the Bears. My mother's first-ever flight was in 1986 when she came with me to Hawaii for the Pro Bowl right after we won the Super Bowl against the New England Patriots.

I attribute my work ethic to my dear mother, Mary, who did so much to please other people, as well as take care of her own family. I hope I was able to please her by the way I conducted my life.

To be able to pay for my mother's trip to Hawaii was very important to me because it represented a tangible example that I made it as a professional athlete and that I could help my family in a direct manner. I mean, it is one thing to satisfy your personal career goal to become a professional football player with all of the bells and whistles that go along with that high-profile profession. But it is quite another major stepping-stone to be able to share your personal success with someone you love.

When the Bears played a game in Atlanta, my mother would come to see me play then because it was close to her home. In fact, even when I was in college at Tennessee State, my mother only came up once to Nashville by car to see me play. It was for my last homecoming game.

Being able to take her with me to Hawaii for the Pro Bowl was one of the most gratifying moments of my life. My mother worked so hard all of her life and experienced so much heartache when it came to trying to raise her family as best she could under trying circumstances. It was time for her to literally smell the roses and smell all of the sweet fragrances of Hawaii, as a symbol of what I had been able to accomplish on her behalf.

I missed taking part in the downtown Chicago parade to celebrate our Super Bowl title that same week. By all accounts, that was a fantastic parade and I wish I could have experienced it with the thousands of Bears fans who braved the freezing cold to attend. But to be with my mother and make her happy and proud meant so much to me. It was her first flight, and it was to one of the most beautiful places in the entire world. I can still recall the aroma from the environment in Hawaii, and I know my mother was so happy.

She told me how happy and proud she was, but she didn't need to say a word. The expression on her face spoke volumes.

For those reasons, I never considered getting involved in anything illegal, especially after achieving my life's goal of reaching the NFL. But I still had a rocky relationship with the Bears organization, and it had to do with trust.

I felt as if I should have been a player the Bears would be proud to promote and showcase. Instead, it seemed, I was always kept in the background, someone they merely tolerated and accommodated.

It hurt me that, after I arrived in the NFL and made it as a dominant defensive player with the Bears, no reporters went back to interview my family to try to learn more about my past. Obviously, if I had been a first-round draft pick, it probably would have been a different story. To me, it just shows how much a team has control of your image, because the Bears never encouraged that kind of story to the media.

The obvious stories are about the first-round draft picks who go on to have success in the NFL. But to me, the better stories are about the underdogs who overcome numerous obstacles in life to not only make an NFL roster, but also manage to excel over the course of their careers. That was my story, and I continue to write new chapters year after year after year.

As players, you know where you stand in the pecking order from the viewpoint of coaches and management. And when you see that the team is not promoting you and not focusing on you the way you want to be accepted, that creates a little bit of a problem. You see, it's all about respect.

Invariably, professional athletes are driven, inspired and motivated by their egos, personal pride and sense of self-worth. Sure, superior talent is evident at this level. You cannot survive in this league without that God-given talent. But there is something more at work in this select environment that separates one player from another.

Even when Walter Payton retired before the 1988 season, and eventually when Steve McMichael, Mike Singletary, Dan Hampton and all the other stars departed, I wondered if Bears coaches and management would consider anointing me as the focal point and leader of the team. Was it going to be my time? Are you going to pass the belt to me? The answer was no. It passed to Tom Waddle, it passed to Jim Harbaugh, it passed to Chris Zorich. You know, give me a break. It's nothing against those particular guys, but my point is I had earned more respect.

I had earned more respect by my actions, not simply my words. I had been productive on the field of play year in and year out on one of the most dominating defenses of all-time. Not only had I produced sacks, quarterback hurries and tackles, but I also had helped make the job easier for my teammates behind me at the linebacker positions and in the secondary. When the men up front put pressure on the quarterback consistently, linebackers can blitz more and cornerbacks and safeties can gamble more to get interceptions.

Here you have an 8th-round draft pick (me) that was paid only $80,000

Mike Ditka (L) and Michael McCaskey summoned me into a meeting during a bye week in my second year in the league. I thought they were going to compliment me on having a break-out season and possibly give me a raise. Instead, I was accused of selling and using drugs by some unknown person who apparently called the Bears offices. I was stunned, angry and humiliated. (Photo courtesy of Mike Kinyon)

and turned into a Pro Bowl player who led the league in sacks back-to-back years and won the Super Bowl MVP. Then you still have issues with this player? There was something dramatically wrong. When you lead the league for two years in a row and there is never any acknowledgement, the writing is on the wall.

So I already knew that this wasn't working for me. I just knew they wanted to see this situation with me go downhill and go sour so they wouldn't have to spend the money they needed to spend.

The management culture in the NFL is very defensive when it comes to admitting a mistake. General managers and scouts spend an inordinate block of time, money and energy evaluating college players all over the country. In essence, that is their life and their passion. If a great player falls through the cracks of their intense and complicated scrutiny, it can be an embarrassment to their system that they were not able to predict with a greater degree of certainty what a player of my pedigree could become.

After my second year with the Bears, I was playing well and producing consistently. We had a bye week and I came back from it to get ready for the next game. In an unusual circumstance, I was summoned upstairs to the executive offices at Halas Hall. Considering how well I had been playing, I viewed this as an encouraging sign.

I walked into the office of general manager Jerry Vainisi. I looked around the office and saw our team owner Michael McCaskey, coach Mike Ditka, and trainer Fred Caito. I had just started the last 10 games of the season and I was kicking ass, doing great, feeling pretty good about myself and the way my football career seemed to be headed. I said, " What s going on? Are you guys giving me a raise, or what?"

They said, "No raise."

So I said, "What's going on?"

They said, "Well, you know, we've got a problem here."

I said, "What's the problem?"

They told me they had some caller who was saying that I was dealing drugs, selling cocaine, or whatever.

I said, "What? You've got to be f_____ kidding!"

I didn't mean to curse, but that's how strongly I felt.

Then I said, "My mom didn't raise me this way. You know what? I'm out of here!"

I went to walk out the door but McCaskey stopped me in order to provide further explanation. I looked back at the guys in the room and said, "Hold on. Who is this person who called?"

They all said they couldn't tell me who it was.

I finally said, "You're going to tell me that I work for you and somebody calls you and says something bad about me and you are going to believe them? You have to be kidding me."

I was so pissed off. Then they said they needed me to take a drug test, which I at first refused because I found that humiliating. I mean, can you imagine how I felt, knowing that I was totally clean and having to submit to a drug test? I felt as if they already had made up their minds that I was guilty of something. It was clear that they did not trust me and did not want to take my word as the truth. There had to be a better way of going about this, I thought.

I went and talked to respected veteran Bears lineman Jim Osborne and a couple of other trusted guys on the team about the issue and accusations. I really couldn't get a good answer about which approach I should take next. I called the league and the NFL Players Union. I found out that a player's contract with a team stipulated that the Bears, or any other team, could demand that you take a drug test at any time, based solely on their suspicions.

I still felt like I was playing very well and yet the Bears were trying to suppress me. Instead of trusting me and encouraging me on and off the field, they continued to throw obstacles in my way when it came to my development. So I surrendered and took the test, however demeaning it felt at the time. Then, in a subsequent team meeting, Ditka gave me a thumbs up, indicating that everything was OK regarding the test results. I said to myself, "Hell, I know everything is OK."

I still felt that these guys were trying to take me out, diminish what I had accomplished to that point as a player and a person. What their motivation was for doing this to me was unclear, yet their actions were undeniable.

After I left that meeting, I went to a nice restaurant/bar in Schaumburg, just north of Chicago. I came out of there and went to a bar in Northbrook to have a beer, to relax by myself. A guy that I didn't know tapped me on the shoulder. I turned around and he shook my hand. As he shook my hand, he put a small plastic container of cocaine in my hand. Now, I wasn't quite sure what it was at first, but I looked at it intently. I put it back in his hand and I looked at him.

I said, "Dude, I am going to turn around. And if I turn back around and I see you, I am going to beat your ass all over this place."

I turned back around and I couldn't find him.

Here's what was going through my mind: I had just gotten off practice and meetings with the Bears and I was pissed off about something they were trying to pin on me. The next thing I knew, somebody walks up to me with some drugs, which had never happened before and has never happened since. So I was very, very pissed.

This all happened in 1984. Four years later, the Bears tried the same tactic, trying to bring me down with drug accusations. And that's when I ended up going to court to fight it.

The NFL at that time had very inconsistent rules in place when it came to testing players for illegal drug use. The league rather arbitrarily subjected certain players to testing without specific guidelines.

In late September 1988, our trainer, Fred Caito, said he had gotten a letter from the league with a list of players they wanted to get tested for drugs and other illegal substances. Now, I came into the league clean, and I don't drink that heavily I don't take a lot of medicine, so I know that has never been a problem. And I don't do drugs, so that's not a problem. Yet, somehow, my name was on this list. I later learned that the Bears had possession of this list in early August.

Caito showed me the list and I cussed him out.

I said, "I was a kid the first time when you dealt me this crap. This time you are dealing with a grown man."

I remember there was a white player on the Bears who got special treatment regarding this drug test, and they didn't go public on him with the assertion. The Bears didn't have anything on me regarding a failed test. I told them they had better have a frozen sample on me to take to court that would prove that I am positive with something. If not, I would hire somebody and we would deal with this legally. I believed in standing up for what was right, and I felt I was being railroaded.

that if I meekly submitted to their demands, I would have done a disservice not only to myself, but to other players who came after me. In a figurative sense, NFL players are the property of the teams that select them. But as humans, we all deserve to be treated fairly and without presumption of guilt.

The NFL, of course, denied any racial discrimination regarding the tests. Spokesman Joe Browne said, "The tests are number coded and colorblind."

But I felt somebody was after me; somebody wanted my ass. But if I was going to go down, I was going to go down my way. I went straight to court and was back at practice the next day. I was going to go to federal court to get the case heard if need be, because this was something far too important not to pursue. I just remember how sick my mother felt after hearing about these latest accusations, because she had been through so much negative stuff with my brothers years earlier. I knew how that drama felt. There was no way I was going to let my mother down. No way I was going to come to the Bears and do some stupid stuff like they were trying to present to me. They were indirectly trying to harm a woman whom I vowed I would never bring harm to.

I eventually was suspended in 1988 when I refused to take another random drug test. But when my agent, Steve Zucker, challenged the suspension, the NFL lifted it.

Bears President Michael McCaskey issued this statement at the time after I voiced my displeasure with the league's testing policy: "I'm sorry that Richard feels that way. I'm very pleased with the way Richard has conducted himself on and off the field. This was a very difficult time for him and certainly one in which we had to wait for the issue to run its course. We had to support the NFL drug policy."

Also in 1988, Chicago sports attorney and adjunct professor Eldon L. Ham was one of the first attorneys to challenge and change the NFL drug policy in court in the case, Richard Dent v. NFL. This became a landmark case in the history of NFL drug testing policies, and it forced the league along with the cooperation and input from our players association, to come up with a more comprehensive plan.

I am certainly not naïve to the drug abuse problems that exist in all of professional sports and in the general population of America. Everyone is entitled to legal rights. Professional athletes are more high profile than many other people in the community, but that does not mean that athletes should be singled out before the facts are in.

GAINING RESPECT

At first, it seemed as if it was me against the world as far as the Bears organization was concerned.

After all, I knew the only way I could receive proper attention was on the field, because the Bears weren't promoting me the way they were Dan Hampton or some of the other high draft picks.

In 1985, I wanted some sort of financial security from the Bears, some kind of financial insurance to protect my future in case a serious injury ended my career prematurely. Everyone knows football is a risky game when it comes to serious injuries, and I certainly was aware that players can get hurt in training camp. That actually happened to me my first year with the Bears. So I told the Bears they needed to do the right thing by renegotiating my contract. I believed I deserved that protection.

Right before our NFC playoff game against the New York Giants at Soldier Field, my agent came out and said he was considering having me sit out the following year if we didn't have a new contract. That put a lot of pressure on me because I was afraid that if we didn't win that Giants game, it would be considered my fault for being a distraction and causing controversy.

Fortunately, we won the game convincingly, 21-0. Our entire defense was overwhelming again against the Giants. We weren't going to lose on my dime; it wasn't going to be because of me.

Still, when contract talks resumed, Bears general manager Jerry Vainisi told me that I would never make more money than Jim McMahon. That's what they thought about me. I felt like I was as much of a game-changer as McMahon or any other quarterback. In today's NFL game, top-notch pass-rushers get paid as much as quarterbacks because of the impact they can have on a game. I was ahead of my time in terms of performance on the field, but I was behind the times in terms of being compensated for what I was worth.

I wanted to be paid like the top pass-rushers of that time were making – somewhere in the neighborhood of $700,000 to $800,000 a year. That seemed reasonable.

So I said to Vainisi: "What is this? Is this slavery?"

He said: "Call it whatever you want to."

I said: "If I can't work for you, I can't work for anybody, right?"

He said: "Call it whatever you want to call it."

I had sat out the Bears' spring mini-camp in 1985 because they had offered me a modest increase to the $300,000-$500,000 range. I took that time to vacation on a cruise ship- the SS Norway-along with several venerable sports celebrities, including famed boxing trainer Angelo Dundee and former NFL greats Ray Nitschke and Art Donovan. In fact, it was Nitschke, the former Packers linebacker, who told me that I could one day become a Hall of Fame player if I continued to perform to my potential. It was great to hear that from a guy who grew up in the Chicago area himself and went on to become a Hall of Fame middle linebacker for Green Bay.

Donovan, who was a Hall of Fame tackle with the old Baltimore Colts, was a fascinating personality. One memory of Donovan that sticks out was watching him eat a bologna sandwich in this fancy dining area aboard our cruise ship.

In the meantime, my talks with the Bears to restructure my contract continued unsuccessfully, and I sat out part of the summer training camp in Platteville, Wisconsin. The Bears wouldn't budge in offering a solid, competitive salary based on what I had already accomplished.

Then I told my agent to get creative by including performance incentives in my contract. One of the incentives was for being named MVP of a Super Bowl. That probably sounded like a far-fetched possibility to the Bears at that time.

When I won that award, the contract stipulated that I receive a bonus of $250,000. Management was ecstatic about our winning the Super Bowl, but I can't imagine they were very happy about forking over an extra quarter of a million dollars to me.

Still, I knew I had to continue proving myself on the field.

My Love-Hate Relationship with Ditka 2

One of the most conflicted relationships I had during my NFL career was with my head coach, Mike Ditka.

It would be amazing if I had been accepted by Ditka. Who knows what I could have done. Instead, I felt like I was fighting my way into a fire every day and trying to stay cool. Imagine what I could have done, who knows?

Ditka had been a Hall of Fame player as a tight end with the Bears, Cowboys and Eagles. As a member of the 1963 Bears, his team won the NFL Championship game against the Giants by a score of 14-10 at Wrigley Field. The first Super Bowl wasn't until 1967, so the NFL Championship game represented the world championship at that time.

A first-round draft pick out of the University of Pittsburgh, Ditka was one of the prototypes of the position, who blocked hard, caught passes and epitomized one of the Monsters of the Midway, as the Bears were known. He was born in the steel town of Aliquippa, Pennsylvania, and his father had been a strict military man.

After serving as an assistant coach for the legendary Tom Landry of the Cowboys, Ditka was named head coach of the Bears as one of the final major decisions of club owner George Halas.

Ditka could be inspirational, influential and obstinate. And more than anything, he often could be confrontational, whether it was with fans, media, players or other coaches.

We won a lot of games during my career with the Chicago Bears, claimed the franchise's only Super Bowl championship, talked a lot of smack, and captured the attention of the city, if not the entire world during the mid-1980s and early 1990s.

But there were many times when Ditka and I clashed, times when I felt he crossed the line of simply trying to motivate me as a player. At the height of our disagreements, Ditka began referring to me as Robert Dent when he spoke to the media. To me, that was the ultimate disrespect. When you purposely mess with someone's real name … that tells me you have no respect for the person. I did not appreciate that at all. But what could I do about it? If I had complained to the media, the story would have garnered more attention and made me feel even more awkward and embarrassed. I felt I was in a no-win situation, even though it was clear I was not happy about this.

There were other times when he would criticize my performances, even though I was giving the Bears unbelievable production. One time I just told Ditka: "If you think you can find somebody else to do what I am doing, then get rid of me! Trade me away!"

Ditka would bark back at me, but I think he knew I had a special talent that would be difficult to replace.

They wouldn't trade me. I just had to continue to take the abuse. I was very disappointed that I did not hear directly from Ditka or my defensive coordinator with the Bears, Buddy Ryan, to congratulate me on being selected to the Pro Football Hall of Fame. Perhaps I will hear something from them at a later date, but I would be surprised if I did.

I know Mike Ditka is revered in Chicago, and he has done many wonderful things for charities and non-profit organizations over the years. He was referred to as Sybil by many of us Bears players because of his multiple personalities. I wish our relationship had been more solid, because in the end, we wanted the same thing. We wanted the Bears to win championships, and we wanted me to play the very best that I could. I know that I was giving it my best shot, always trying to figure out the strategies of opposing offenses.

I always felt that opposing offenses had to account for my being on the field, whether it meant commanding a double-team block or deliberately running a play away from where I lined up.

All of us want to be respected by our peers and by the people we report to at the end of the day. For that reason, I constantly sought to receive positive reinforcement from Buddy Ryan, as well as Ditka and my teammates on defense.

I knew that I had a strike against me coming into the NFL because I was an 8th-round draft pick from a small school in Tennessee. Could I ever overcome those long odds? Would I ever be recognized and judged simply by my production on the field and not by my pedigree? Those were questions I had to ask myself throughout my NFL career.

Despite the success and high profile nature of the Bears, especially after we won the Super Bowl, there still were groups of players and coaches who did not necessarily like each other. That's just the way it goes in any organization. Dan Hampton and Jim McMahon probably didn't like each other, for instance. They sniped at each other through the media, especially Hampton.

Dan Hampton, shown here, was a first-round draft pick of the Bears who would wind up in the Pro Football Hall of Fame. Despite enduring numerous surgeries, particularly on his knees, he was a major contributor as both a defensive end and tackle. Hampton sometimes questioned the toughness of our frequently-injured quarterback, Jim McMahon. (Photo courtesy of Mike Kinyon)

Everybody wants to be the so-called glory guy, the player that everyone admires and focuses on as being indispensable. So sometimes a little resentment and jealousy will creep in and disrupt the good vibes that a team otherwise would share. You can sense the uncomfortable negative feelings, and you can watch them fester. But when it came to game time for us, we had to get our job done and put aside petty feelings. We had to let go of the individual egos and do what was best for the team.

Hampton, a Hall of Fame defensive lineman who was a first-round draft pick out of Arkansas, often questioned the toughness of McMahon, who missed some important post-season games because of injuries. McMahon's leadership and skill were sorely missed in some of those tough losses in the late 1980s. But we also knew that McMahon had taken a physical beating back there, including one that led to a serious kidney injury.

One time in particular, in 1986, the Packers' Charles Martin slammed McMahon to the ground well after McMahon had released the pass.

We were as incredulous about what we just saw on the field as the fans in the stadium and the millions of folks watching the game on television were. There are times such as that when teams bond and really separate personal feelings for teammates.

But there always will be disagreements within a team, whether it's football, basketball, baseball, hockey, or any other high-profile team sport.

In fact, it was no secret that Ditka and Buddy Ryan often feuded. We all remember when they had to be separated at halftime of our game in Miami that turned out to be our only loss of the 1985 season. They argued about whether we should be blitzing more, and they disagreed about the fact that we were not trying to run more on offense. It is during times of stress that the true character of an individual is revealed.

It seemed that their rift may have affected the chemistry between our offensive and defensive players. Ryan was carried off the field by several of our defensive players at the end of Super Bowl XX in New Orleans and Ditka was carried off by others.

It was interesting to see Ditka invite Ryan back to Chicago in 2010 for our 25-year anniversary celebration of the Super Bowl championship. The two coaches seemed to bury the hatchet at that stage of their lives, especially after it was revealed publicly that Ryan was suffering from cancer.

Similar to any family unit that experiences discord and occasional disagreement, we soldiered on and remained confident that we would accomplish our ultimate goal.

There were some guys on that Bears team who thought we might be jinxing ourselves by prematurely performing in the "Super Bowl Shuffle." We taped it even before the regular season was over in 1985. Willie Gault, Gary Fencik, Mike Richardson, Otis Wilson, Mike Singletary, Jim McMahon,

Whether I was on the playing field or watching intently from the sideline, I always considered myself a smart observer of the game of football. My patience was tested often with the Bears, especially as a younger player waiting for my opportunity to be anointed as a leader based on my dominant performances on the field. (Photo courtesy of Mike Kinyon)

Steve Fuller, William Perry, Walter Payton … we all thought it was a great idea, and we all had the confidence in our team to eventually back up our words with a Super Bowl championship. It proved to be a great motivator, and sure enough, we pretty much coasted through the playoffs that year.

We dispatched the Giants, Rams, and Patriots in unprecedented fashion and didn't look back.

What came so smoothly and naturally on the field during the 1985 season belied the awkwardness and disconnected feeling I had when I first joined the Bears two years earlier.

It took me awhile to really feel accepted by my new teammates. I mean, guys noticed my exceptional performances in the one-on-one practice drills. They could see me running by Jim Covert, a first-round draft pick at offensive left tackle. And they could see me running by Noah Jackson and Dan Jiggetts and whoever else was lined up against me on the offensive line. Once they got in their stance, if they didn't pop out of it quickly, I was past them.

So the confidence was building for me from that standpoint. But I was still shy and I really didn't feel as if I was fitting in properly. That was, to some extent at least, just part of being a rookie, I guess. Veteran players don't just automatically allow you into their inner circle or their fraternity. You have to earn that respect over a period of time to get that appreciation. Eventually I think I got some grudging respect over time, at least from the players. But I still was not being respected by some of the coaches and management.

Here's an example of what I am talking about: I was with the Bears for 10 years, was MVP of the Super Bowl, and yet I was never named captain of the team over that period of time. I knew I was making shit happen. I knew it was my team. At some point, I should have been named captain. I was very disappointed that during my career and my entire time that I was with Mike Ditka … he never gave me the team as a captain.

Was it Walter Payton's team when I first got there? Yes. When Walter left after 1987, I guess I just wasn't the *Chosen One* that the team wanted to get behind. When Mike Singletary left a few years later, OK, I thought, maybe this would be my time. When Dan Hampton left, OK, was it my time yet? Give me the team!

I was a leader in college. I called the plays on defense for two years, so I knew and I appreciated the game. But to me it was always an uphill battle with the Bears organization. They wanted to give the team leadership to Jim Harbaugh, they wanted to give it to Tom Waddle, they wanted to give it to Chris Zorich, they wanted to give it to Ron Rivera. I was the one who was going to make those guys better, if you put the light on me and let me shine. I knew that at the end of the day, those other players still were going to turn around and look at me and say: 'Let's go!'

That part made me feel bitter; it felt bad. It made me feel like: *'What? I'm not good enough for you people?' You won't let me go to another team. So at the end of the day, let me go. Don't keep me here. Don't screw up my life.* That's the way I looked at it. When I was negotiating my contract and Jerry Vainisi told me I would never make more than Jim McMahon, I had to think: *OK, what's that about? Because he's a quarterback I can't make more? But yet I am producing more. Because he is making $700,000 or $800,000, I can't make $700,000 or $800,000?*

That was wrong.

I realized early on that professional football is a business to the extent that organizations choose who they want to represent them. There's a lot of politics involved and that's what young kids don't know today. You may have all the talent in the world, but the organizations just want you there for a certain length of time. You are there until they find your replacement. When I first arrived on the scene with the Bears, I felt like I was creating a problem for the organization because they had other players they were intending to pay the big money. This happens across the league, not just here in Chicago. They wanted Al Harris and Dan Hampton to be the guys to pay the big money to. But I was the one pushing them. They had no money invested in me. They had more of an investment in those other guys. So that was a problem to me.

I should have been drafted higher than the 8th round. But management will never say that they made a mistake. I often say rejection is God's protection. That's reality. It's God's way of saying it is time to move on. Things happen for a reason.

All the while as a rookie, I watched and observed what was going on, trying to soak in things like a sponge. I did the same in college. I tried to stay in place, work hard, and hoped to get noticed as a difference-maker of a player. Initially I was allowed to play on third-down passing situations with the Bears. I wanted to win and I wanted to be a part of our team's success. I knew I could do the job if given the chance.

When I was on the sideline, I was constantly in the ear of Buddy Ryan, begging him to let me get in the game.

At our first practice scrimmage, I think I had about three sacks. I mainly was going against left tackle Jim Covert. I was running right by their first-rounder. I felt like I was getting somewhere. Now I knew that I had to take this same aggression, technique, and performance into an actual game. What I had done to my own teammate, I had to take that to an actual game. For me, I knew that if I had been given enough repetitions in practice, I would be able to make something happen. It was all about getting out there and getting some reps. I knew I could make it happen.

In my first preseason game, I made some things happen. I tipped the ball and caused an interception, and I got some hits. Later in the game, I got a lot of reps because Buffalo was behind and the Bills sent my former Tennessee State roommate in at guard, a guy named Darryl Caldwell. They sent him into the game to try to slow me down. I yelled out to him, "Oh, home boy. Just like old times, right? We just went through this about five months ago." He was one of my best friends in college, and here I ended up competing in my first NFL game against him.

It turned out to be one of those surrealistic moments in my life. It helped me realize how far I had come, yet it still kept me grounded in terms of remembering my past.

The next week I was feeling great, and all of us rookies were having a good time. We were in practice and Jimbo Covert and Mark Bortz rolled up on my left ankle and my foot went out from under me. I did a split. Bortz and whoever was on him ran on top of me, as well as the center and Jimbo. So I've got about four guys on top of me as I did the splits, and I snapped my hamstring and rolled up on my ankle. I was shot.

So now I couldn't do anything for three weeks. I was a little pissed because I knew the cycle in the NFL once you get injured, especially as a young player. They cut you. You get back half-way healthy, they get you on the film not performing at 100 percent and you get cut. So I was going to make sure I didn't come back too early to play poorly on film. All I was trying to do was get healthy. I couldn't even sit on the toilet. When I sat on the toilet, I had to extend by left leg because I couldn't bend it. And it would take me close to 10 minutes just to walk to my car. Those first two or three days I had to take baby steps because my left ankle and right hamstring were shot.

Finally, I got to the point after a couple of weeks where I knew I could play again. But to what level, I wasn't sure. I knew it wasn't going to be at the same level that I walked into camp performing. But I wanted to contribute again as soon as possible. I had some speed still, but I couldn't get that knee up as high as I wanted to.

So, I decided to consult with Jim Osborne, Noah Jackson, Emery Moorehead and some of the other veterans. These were guys that I kind of trusted because they had been in the league for a long time. What should I do? Moorehead said something that registered with me. He said, "Look, man, you've been getting past that first-rounder ever since you have been here. I don't think you have anything to worry about. Those folks know what you can do. I think you are already on the team. You just have to get yourself healthy and get ready."

I thought about it and wondered if I should try to go out and play. Maybe play on special teams or something like that. If they ask me to go out there and give everything for five seconds, I can do that. I can do that well. So I went out there and did that and, boom! I was on the team.

We opened up the regular season against Atlanta and I had a chance to block a punt. We lost the game, and our special teams coach, Steve Kazor, tried to make it sound as if we had lost because I didn't stretch out to block the punt. I said, "You've got to be kidding. If that's what you want to say, that's cool." I also got to play on third downs early in the season. But by the end of the season, we weren't going anywhere as a team, so the coaches wanted to see what we might be able to do in 1984. They started me at defensive end the last two games. One of the games was in Philadelphia, I believe, and then we came home for that last game against Green Bay.

The wind-chill was 48 degrees below. Oh, my God! That was a real eye-opener for me. It taught me that you can't worry about the weather, because Mother Nature is going to do her thing regardless. It's mind over matter. It wasn't as if the powers that be were going to call the game off like they do in baseball. Everyone just had to deal with the elements.

It was so cold that we decided to cut down the time in the pregame warmups. When we came back into the locker room, I remember sitting there, looking at my hands frozen solid. Next thing I knew, one of the referees knocked on the door to our locker room and yelled, "Two minutes, Coach. Two minutes!"

That's when I realized that I had to go back and spend three hours out there. Now my mind is just racing. How in the world was I going to be able to do that? It seemed as if I could hear conversations in the crowd that you don't normally hear. That was because the fans were trying to deal with the frigid temperatures, as well. Players had icicles on their beards and mustaches.

At halftime, I remember our general manager, Bill Tobin, came in and said, What's the matter with you? You looked terrible out there. I said: Hey, man, it's cold out there. That was my first taste of extremely cold weather in the Midwest. Throughout that whole off-season, my toes tingled from that experience with frostbite. I never wanted to see another day like that.

DITKA'S FIRING

One of the historic days in Chicago sports occurred when Ditka was fired after the 1992 season. He began his farewell speech by saying: "I'll try to do this with class, I don't know if I can. Scripture tells you that all things shall pass. This, too, shall pass. Regrets? Just a few, but too few to remember. I can't sing it quite as good as he could (referring to Frank Sinatra)." After thanking his assistant coaches and praising key players on the team, including Walter Payton, Ditka finished by saying: "This, too, shall pass."

It was an emotional day for him, and fans of the Bears seemed to be in mourning. But we players knew we still had a job to do, and now our future careers were on the line.

Ditka coached the Bears for 11 seasons before being fired. In 1997, he returned to coaching with the New Orleans Saints for a period he later referred to as the "three worst years" of his life. He was fired as the Saints coach after going 15-33.

Ditka was criticized after he traded all of the Saints' 1999 draft picks, plus their first-round draft pick in 2000, to the Washington Redskins to move up in the draft and select Texas running back Ricky Williams. The bold move failed to produce immediate dividends.

Over a total of 14 seasons as an NFL head coach, Ditka had a regular-season record of 121-95 and a postseason mark of 6-6. He coached the Bears to six NFC Central titles and three trips to the NFC Championship. And of course, Ditka also coached the Bears when we whipped the New England Patriots, 46-10, in Super Bowl XX.

Ditka was known for his short temper with the media and fans.

One of the most famous exchanges Ditka had with the media occurred when the team was struggling in 1990.

Ditka and the late Red Mottlow, who was a veteran radio sportscaster for WFYR-FM at the time, really got into an argument one Monday morning. Ditka was holding his press conference on December 10, 1990, in the basement of the old Halas Hall, and he was in an especially foul mood after a 10-9 loss at Washington.

The press conference was cut short after six minutes. It ended as Ditka said to Mottlow: "I always try to appease a jerk."

Then Mottlow replied: "You're a double one."

That argument was precious. It sounded like the ones we had as kids growing up in the neighborhood. But that was often the way you communicated with Ditka.

Not Feeling the Love 3

I never was made to feel I was the *Chosen One*.

Everyone likes to feel special or privileged. Whether that means in a family setting or as a member of a football team, it's comforting to know that someone thinks you are full of promise.

From the time I was a child growing up with eight siblings in a small, crowded house in Atlanta, to the time I became an 8th-round draft pick of the Chicago Bears in 1983, I always felt as if I had to go the extra mile to prove myself, to get noticed. And even after I felt I had proven myself worthy of the adulation and rewards that I sought, my patience often was tested before I finally benefited.

No doubt that was the case when my pro football career ended – a career that saw me become the Bears all-time leader in quarterback sacks. I was the third all-time leader in sacks in the entire NFL at the time of my retirement in 1996. Yet it took eight agonizing times of falling short of enough votes before I was finally selected for the Pro Football Hall of Fame in 2011.

Once again I felt helpless and overlooked. I would be lying if I said it didn't hurt me to fall short of the Hall of Fame so many times. I didn't play the game of football initially with the idea of making the Hall of Fame. I just loved the game and I knew that I could excel and hopefully be good enough to make a living in the NFL. Well, I exceeded those basic expectations and

Growing up in Georgia with seven brothers and one sister, I learned early that I had to compete for attention from my parents. I tried my best to steer clear of trouble, even though there seemed to be trouble all around me. My overwhelming goal was to make my mother proud of me.

crafted some pretty impressive numbers that stack up with the best of them at my position. I felt it was my time finally to get rewarded.

It was a long time coming when I finally broke the barrier in 2011. It was well worth the wait. I guess this is my shining time. Finally, my shining time.

I was forced to learn how to be patient a long, long time ago. There were a lot of directions to turn during my childhood and teenage years. Frighteningly, most of those directions would have landed me in deep trouble if I had continued down those paths. It took time, faith, and a bit of good fortune to allow me to wind up where I am today.

Gangs, drugs, other criminal activity … all of those negative paths were all around me and beckoning young men of my background and circumstance and who were without positive direction or purpose.

I grew up in the East Lake and Kirkwood communities: the last neighborhoods before you get out of Fulton County in Georgia. I went to East Lake Elementary School, and our family's place of worship was Beulah Baptist Church. I vividly remember playing around with my brothers back in the early1960s. It was an innocent time when we were grateful for what we had and weren't really aware of what was missing from our daily lives.

I grew up with seven brothers and one sister, and all of us are one year apart in age. My late mother's name was Mary; my dad's name is Horace. Early in my life, both of my parents were there for us, working hard to get us out of the projects.

I remember when we moved from Kirkwood to East Lake. That was some serious time in the projects. I also remember all of us screwing around as little kids, playing in water during the scorching summers in the Atlanta area. That was our idea of fun, and it was pretty crazy. You see, our parents didn't have the time, money or inclination to provide us with any structured entertainment or neighborhood activities at that time. We were pretty much on our own to find something to do.

Similar to the childhoods of many of us, there were myths, local folklore, and embellishments. For instance, I remember our idea of the boogeyman when I was a kid was someone known locally as The Green Man. We just knew we didn't want to be caught by him. Looking back now, he probably was quite harmless.

I never was quite sure who this mysterious man was and why he unwittingly caused so much fear among the children in our neighborhood. This was an era that preceded intense local scrutiny of strangers who passed through our local turf. Our parents simply allowed us to go outside and play, without the many caution flags that come with the territory nowadays when instructing children.

I can still envision the modest house where I grew up. It had a living room, dining room, two bedrooms, and one bathroom for the entire family. It amazes me now that all of us lived in that house all the way up to my sophomore year in high school. Then we moved into Decatur, Georgia, to a place called Eastwick Village. My mom had lost the house at that time because of financial hardship. My parents' divorce had taken place, and it definitely was a tough time for all of us. I also have one sister and a half-brother. Their names are Brenda Anderson and Neal Anderson, not to be confused with the former Chicago Bears running back of the same name.

My other brothers were Horace Jr., George, Jerome, Johnny, Steve, and James.

My dad buffed floors for a living, and I also remember seeing him work as a security man. Sometimes I would accompany him, which turned out to be very enlightening for a youngster, as we would buff a lot of floors around the Atlanta and Decatur area. We buffed the floors of office buildings and hospitals. My father taught me how to use a large buffer and walk it around a room when he would get those night jobs. It may not sound like the most exciting activity in the world, but it was a great bonding time for me and my dad. As I look back on that experience now, I realize that he was the security man for a lot of buildings, as well as receiving extra money for cleaning the floors.

I also have fond memories of doing a lot of fishing with my dad. I remember one time around 1968 when he and I went fishing on a typically hot afternoon in the South. After fishing, we were in the car getting ready to leave, and that's when we were confronted by a state trooper who had pulled up. He wanted to see our fishing license. My dad's license had expired, and the trooper said he had to take us down to the police station. My dad told the trooper that he didn't want to have any of his kids exposed to a legal situation like that. He wanted to drop me off at home before driving to the station.

Well, the trooper would not go for this arrangement and insisted that my dad immediately follow him to the station in Covington, Georgia. At that time, Covington was not a nice place to be for African-Americans.

My father started following the policeman, but when the trooper made a turn, my father kept going straight and took off fast. I just remember looking out the back window as we left the trooper in the dust. There actually was a huge cloud of dust from that dirt road. It seemed like a scene from a movie as we sped away, and I remember it like it was yesterday.

But less than two weeks later, the police came and got him. My father went with them without incident. He just didn't want the police to take him into custody the first time with his kids seeing it happen.

Growing up, I was always considered a momma's boy. All of my brothers were daddy's boys. So my mom wanted me to do things with him whenever possible. It seemed to me that my brothers

My father, Horace (L.) is 78 and my grandfather, Jim (R.) lived to be 93. This photo was taken in 2002. I hope to have similar longevity in my life in spite of what some surveys project for former NFL players. I know I have to take care of my body, eat right and exercise. My goal is to enjoy life to the fullest.

were always competing to get dad's attention. As it turned out, I was the only one in the family who played sports.

My father and I share the same birthday, December 13, so as a kid I thought that I was supposed to grow up to be like him. But with him being an alcoholic and somewhat abusive at that time, I wasn't enjoying that prospect. But I later learned to appreciate the good things he did, and I understood the type of pressure he was under as a black man facing the racial realities in the South.

That is not to make light of his alcoholism and the mistakes he made and surely regrets. Growing up with several siblings in a small house, we all saw and heard a lot of things we probably shouldn't have.

Our family did just about everything to try to get by during some difficult economic times.

My siblings and I were musicians. Well, at least I tried to be. Horace played the bass, George played the drums. Johnny was the so-called "Michael Jackson performer," singing and dancing, and Jerome played the organ. If America's Got Talent had been around at that time, our family certainly would have been a contender.

We used to have what we called Rally Shows around Decatur, and we used to have our own little shows in our back yard, as well. We would charge a quarter to get in. One side of our street was in Fulton County and the other side was Decatur. So we drew fans from both areas.

I didn't have the musical skills to play an instrument in the group with my brothers. I tried playing the bongo drums. But then Johnny came along and played the bongos, danced, sang and did everything. So I was out. We had a cousin, Sap Anderson, who played the guitar. So it was quite competitive among us. And when you look at the money that was split up, there wasn't much to go around.

We lived on Farr Road, and the last house on the corner was my friend Scott Dean's house. His father was a minister, and Scott was an only child. Scott had no TV in his house because his father didn't believe in having one. He was pretty strict. And there was another minister who lived next to the Dean's house; and our neighbor on the other side of our house also was a minister. So we used to refer to our block as Ministers' Row. I often think about how lucky we were to live in the middle of all those ministers. In addition to those ministers, my grandmother was very religious and was quite active at Agnes Scott College. She must have worked there for 40 or 50 years. And she worked at a church in Beulah during the same time.

While my family loved music, we also were into sports. I remember being very young and going out to play football. I just remember my dad yelling at me and criticizing the way I played one particular time, and it made a bad first impression on me. Immediately following that incident, I remember saying to myself that I was done with football. At the age of five or six, I felt that I didn't want to have anything else to do with organized football. But I would continue playing informally around the neighborhood, playing quarterback, fullback or whatever was needed, because I was the biggest guy around.

Before I was in high school, I was still torn as to what direction to follow. You see, I had a bunch of bad-ass brothers who were getting into trouble all the time. Other than the talent they had as musicians, they were tough guys in the neighborhood who sometimes, regrettably, broke the law. Even when I was in the first and second grade, we were doing a lot of things that kids that age, or any age, shouldn't be doing. I didn't have very many good choices to make, it seemed. There was no other world there for me to see.

I remember times when we would walk to the Middle School and some of the tough guys would line up to take money from the younger kids. They would take their money or their meal card, or whatever. We had to learn to grow up quickly, in order to survive. I saw many of the younger kids get bullied by the older boys. Trying to avoid the same fate just added stress to all of our lives.

I was conflicted at the time as to which way to go with my life. Should I try to become a Black Panther and fight for something? Those were angry times, not many positive options. There was a park there for us, but that's all we had. There was no supportive group there providing productive, encouraging guidance for us. You see, I had a chance to see all of my bad-ass brothers, and they were my examples to consider. Everybody knew not to mess with the Dents. I had one brother who spent some serious time in jail.

Organized sports was a way for me to gain acceptance and perhaps escape some of the perils of gangs and thugs and bullies. So I figured that might be my way out of that situation.

My junior year of high school, I was cut from the basketball team. I was stunned, but I hung around and refused to give up. I persevered.

It was my friend Scott Dean who encouraged me to stick with high school football. Scott knew that my dream was to play ball professionally and be able to take care of my mother with some nice things, get her out of that neighborhood, and take her places. It was as if the devil in me wanted to follow the path of my brothers, but the angel in me wanted to do the right thing and pursue a worthwhile goal. Since Scott's father was a minister, Scott was a good person for me to talk to about my future. He was a great person to bounce my feelings off and get a reaction. He wouldn't tell me to do something or not to do something, but he allowed me to vent while he offered kind advice. He allowed me to think out loud, so to speak.

Scott would say, "Pursue your dreams. You can always go back to work, man." When Scott hit me with that advice, it registered with me, because I had to make a move, make a decision. So that was why we went out for spring football together. Scott gave up the band – maybe a little because he wanted a girlfriend, but mostly because I was thinking of quitting school. Scott said to me, "I'll quit the band and play ball with you if you stay" – and he LOVED the band.

So we both went out for football, even though his dad was against sports. When the season started, Scott would walk to my house with a blue band uniform on before switching into his regular gear, just so his folks wouldn't know what he was up to. Eventually they found out he was playing football, and they wouldn't come out to see him play.

I am sure Scott would have loved to have had his parents' approval to play football, but he was accustomed to their strict ways. Later in life Scott's parents found out that he quit the band – they never knew when he was in high school.

In addition to playing football at J.C. Murphy High School, I also played basketball my junior and senior years and made All-City in both sports. But the very first sport I went out for in high school was golf, a sport I continue to tinker with to this day.

I have had the opportunity to play in many celebrity golf tournaments since I have been associated with the Bears. It is a frustrating game, but I can hold my own on the course, and it is just fun to be outside in beautiful surroundings with a group of friends.

My golf handicap today ranges from a 9 to about a 14, depending on the course and circumstances. My favorite golf story involves playing with Michael Jordan and Tiger Woods at the Merit Club in Libertyville, Illinois, in 1997.

Woods had won one of his four Master's tournaments and was in Chicago to appear on the Oprah Show.

The three of us played at least 18 holes, as I recall, then retreated to Jordan's suburban mansion to play some basketball on his outdoor court. This was before he had an indoor court installed.

Anyway, it was me and one of Michael's friends against M.J. and Tiger. We all know how competitive Michael is regardless of what sport he is playing or under what conditions. I always joked that if he ever took a nap, he could run all day.

Tiger and Michael's friend had tennis shoes on, and M.J. and I had socks on while we played basketball. I couldn't move too much, tired from playing golf, but we're playing anyway. Tiger hit a jump shot and I tried to recruit Michael. He is just standing there. I said: "Hey, hack him! Put it on him!"

So on this same day, we had played golf for about six hours, played basketball at Michael's house, and that night M.J. went out and scored 55 points for the Bulls in a playoff game against Washington. It was just amazing what this guy was able to do. For me as an athlete, I know what rest and staying off your feet on the day of a game can mean. I have never seen a human being like Jordan who could do the things he did.

Who could have ever imagined that I would one day be playing golf with Tiger Woods and Michael Jordan after my humble introduction to the sport as a kid?

Meanwhile, there remained serious challenges for me and my family, in part due to my father's alcoholism.

He's over that now, but I am sure that had an effect on his entire life. He has been there for me, yet there is no doubt that I was always a momma's boy.

Watching how hard my mother used to work was heartbreaking at times. She would raise other people's kids, cook, clean, iron and press clothes, fix people's hair, keep their lives together. And not to mention the fact that she would handle my taxes when I was old enough to have a job. She was an amazing person and I miss her dearly to this day.

As I reflect on my life – the decisions that I made, the trials and the tribulations I endured, the successes and failures that I experienced – I have few regrets.

Both personally and professionally, through the game of football I have achieved more than I could have possibly dreamed or imagined as a young boy growing up at-risk in Georgia in the 1960s. As I continue to navigate my way through life at the age of 52, I become more retrospective and maybe even a little more nostalgic. Yet I am even more determined to leave a legacy more meaningful and everlasting than that of simply a Hall of Fame pro football player who was able to sack the quarterback and entertain millions of NFL fans.

In figurative terms, we all are here on this earth for just a minute. Even if you are fortunate enough to live 100 years, that would be a short period of time in the big picture of the earth's existence. But I make no small plans for the rest of my life. I understand that being a Hall of Fame football player provides me a special platform to have other people listen to what I have to say. To that extent, I try to impart the wisdom of my age and experience when I talk to youngsters or aspiring young adults.

The time-honored expression that you have to take time to smell the roses is something I really take to heart. From my days growing up in the South enjoying nature, cutting neighbors' grass, climbing trees, planting seeds, playing water games, enjoying that feeling of accomplishment in the great outdoors … that is my literal meaning of smelling the roses in life.

At my age, I try not to obsess over the commonly-held notion that former pro football players, on average, live shorter lives than those of other Americans. I know that you can't continue to go through life weighing over 300 pounds. You have to take care of yourself, watch what you eat and exercise. We all have some control over that. My grandfather died at age 93 and my dad is still living at 78, so that is encouraging. I can clearly state that I appreciate every moment in time that I have on this earth. That is why we all have to appreciate one another and say the things that need to be said, because you never know what is in store for the future.

In fact, a study released in May of 2012 disputed the previous findings that NFL players live shorter lives than the general population. According to a report in *USA Today*, a study conducted by the National Institute for Occupational Safety and Health (NIOSH) examined the life spans of about 3,439 former NFL players. Of that group, 334 were deceased. The results also showed that almost 38 percent of the deaths of the retirees who played between 1959 and 1988, were the result of heart disease.

Of concern to me, however, was the statistic that showed former defensive linemen had a 42 percent higher risk of death from heart disease when compared to men in the general population. And African-American players have a 69 percent higher chance of dying from heart ailments than white players, the report said.

Whatever the numbers reveal, I know that I have to be diligent about taking care of my body through exercise and smart eating habits.

I want to be around as long as possible to continue to make contributions to society and enjoy my family and friends.

I believe in people, and what turns me on the most is knowing that I am one of those public figures in a unique position to help and inspire someone else to achieve an important goal. That is so fulfilling. No amount of money can replace that feeling I get when I see someone else succeed. I beam with pride when I hear someone else say: "You inspired me to work hard and have confidence in myself to persevere through difficult times to reach my goal."

I was always that kind of guy who battled through adversity to succeed, so I can identify with many people who have to be patient and faithful and persistent to achieve in life.

For the last 10 years I have been in the energy management business. As I oversee my energy-supply business in Chicago, I recall that I was always kind of nerdy when it came to liking technology and energy. As a business-man, I don't feel like I will ever be the one to drop the ball; I am going to get things done. Now I am also a supplier and manager, as well. I have focused on natural gas and energy management issues as the CEO of RLD Resources, LLC. I have tried to educate consumers about ways to save natural gas and save on energy costs. There are so many basic things that residents can do to save heating costs in the wintertime, including providing adequate insulation in their attics.

I manage to keep quite busy with a variety of initiatives. In addition to my involvement in leading the Make a Dent Foundation, I have also served on the board of the Better Boys Foundation and the Illinois Literacy Program, and I am a business partner in Harry Caray's Italian Steakhouse in Chicago.

PERSONAL FOULS AND TRIUMPHS

When it comes to understanding the women in my life, everything starts with the early appreciation and observation of my own mother. I respected her so much for what she did daily, not only for our family, but for all of the other families that she helped. While growing up, I wasn't able to fully comprehend all that she did as much as I did when I became an adult.

My first girlfriend's name was Sherry, and we dated in the 11th grade at Murphy High School. You really don't know what you are doing at that age. It can be an awkward, clumsy period for anyone that age as you learn the give-and-take of a relationship and how to make it last. Later on in high school, I dated a girl named Margaret who had beautiful dark brown skin. She was very cool, very smart, and she was a cheerleader.

I met a lot of girls in summer school, and it did not take me long to realize that being a member of the football team certainly helped my popularity with the girls. We went to movies, roller skating parties and local music events, things of that nature. There is no question that the notoriety athletes receive jacks up their popularity to the highest level, and I was enjoying every minute of that.

Football was so much a time-consuming priority in my life in college, but we did find time to party and enjoy the company of beautiful women. But nothing serious ever resulted.

Once I became a professional football player, I met my future wife, Leslie, in 1987 in Atlanta. She was getting her master's degree at Georgia Tech at the time. I had a good feeling right away that this relationship was going to be something special. We used to talk about a lot of things and we did a lot together, but our careers took us separate ways for a period of time before we reconnected. A year went by that we had lost touch, and after I got back to Chicago to prepare for the next season with the Bears, the phone number I thought I had for her was all screwed up.

Later in 1988, the Bears practiced down in Atlanta. I had an injured ankle at the time, but I was still around the team. I remember attending an NBA game involving the Atlanta Hawks and I happened to see Leslie there at the game. I signaled to her that I couldn't walk up stairs because of my ankle injury, so she came down to where I was sitting. We talked and I explained to her about the phone number mix-up as we caught up on a lot of things. I decided to invite her to my mother's house in the Atlanta area for dinner with me and a lot of my Bears teammates. I wanted her to get a chance to meet my mom. Everything went well, and it was like Leslie and I had never lost touch. We had a very good time there. I drove her home and we remained in contact after that.

Many NFL observers had reported that the most athletic play I made in 1988 was when I soared over a blocker and sacked San Francisco 49ers quarterback Joe Montana during a nationally-televised Monday Night game that we won 10-9 at Soldier Field. But I felt as if I had made a pretty impressive move off the field at the time when I reconnected with Leslie that year.

She would come to Chicago on occasion and we began growing even closer. I knew what the potential was as far as the relationship. I proposed to her in Chicago after I had bought her a new coat and placed the engagement ring in one of the pockets. We got married in 1990.

Marriage is a great experience; it is a great partnership. She was trying to find out what was the next best thing to do, and I was enjoying success in football. There is nothing better than having someone to share your success. Leslie became an attorney in Chicago.

Unfortunately, we went our separate ways. We divorced in 2003. Leslie gave me two little girls – Mary and Sarah – and raised them. The girls wanted to be with their mother following the divorce. I hardly can contain the pride

I have in my two daughters. It is difficult for me to fathom that they have grown so quickly into beautiful, responsible and enterprising young women. Mary is a senior at Valparaiso University, where she plays volleyball. And Sarah is a sophomore at Marquette University. I am so proud of the fact that my girls are finishing college, which I did not.

Sarah wants to be like her grandmother; she likes the restaurant business. She wants to own her own restaurant and she wants to serve people. She has that service attitude and personality. I am so proud of how both of them have turned out.

Mary, my first child, was named after my mother, and I remember taking her to my mother's grave site. She has a lot of the same qualities my mother had, including being a very giving person. She is always ready to help and support others. It is amazing how she has matured.

Their mother did well in raising them. And I tried to show them as much as I could in terms of letting them meet all kinds of people from various backgrounds. The girls know who they are, where they came from, and where they are going.

I think Mary is more of an analytical type, more like a lawyer, as is her mother. Sarah is kind of like me in terms of her personality. If she is not talking, then she is not happy and something is wrong. If Mary is quiet, you can't say that something is necessarily wrong, because that's sort of her personality. She is kind of laid-back and always analyzing things. She is very smart and very inquisitive.

Both of my girls have been able to establish their own identities away from the celebrity that I earned as a professional football player. I am proud that they are associated with the foundation that has my name and their grandmother's name. The girls seem to be able to find their own way in life. I look forward to them being able to extend the many accomplishments of our foundation over the years. Sometimes marriages don't work out, but you are still family. The divorce was tough for me to go through. I was coaching that year as an assistant with the Bears. Keeping busy during that time helped me get through the divorce and bounce back.

I signed my divorce papers on my birthday, December 13, making it even tougher.

One of the stresses on my marriage to Leslie was an allegation from a woman from Mississippi who had sent me a letter claiming that I had fathered her son.

The woman who made this paternity accusation kept referencing that she met me in a coffee shop over a period of several days in Mississippi. I don't drink coffee and I don't carry a pager. I said: "I don't know who you are."

I didn't want to worry Leslie about this accusation, so I did not tell her initially. It's unfortunate how sometimes when you don't tell someone close to you something important, it can come back to bite you in the ass.

This strange letter was sent to me sometime around 1993. This woman and I ended up talking to each other back and forth on the phone. I kept telling her that the father of her son was not me.

By 2003, this mysterious woman had moved to Texas and insisted that I take a paternity test, in accordance with that state's law. I was served a subpoena while I was at a Bears' practice. At that point, I decided to talk to Leslie about the situation. But at that juncture, Leslie and I already were having problems in the marriage, so this paternity allegation was just another problem on top of our other marital concerns.

I went to get the paternity test and it came back negative, as I knew it would. This incident reinforced in me that someone from the outside can bring drama into your home, even if you don't know that person. But the fact that I did not talk to Leslie initially about this accusation in 1993, made it difficult ten years later in 2003. And with Leslie being an attorney, I have to believe that she had heard through her sources that something was going on with regard to this paternity charge against me. She never brought it up to me.

I had made a judgment call back in '93 that it wasn't a good thing to tell my wife about something I didn't want to deal with. It was my decision at that time not to stress her out because she was on bedrest with our second child.

But when everything came to light ten years later, it simply wasn't a good time in our marriage to try to get through yet another crisis.

Sadly, it was time to move on for both of us.

I met R.J.'s mother when I was going through my divorce. I think she was dating or seeing someone on that current Bears team at that time. I thought she was

My young son, R.J., is my pride and joy. Here we are shown enjoying a movie premier. Life can be especially difficult for young black kids. My fervent desire is for him to have a decent opportunity to become all that he is capable of achieving.

modeling and doing other stuff like that. I did not monitor or investigate that situation like I should have, as I had done in previous relationships. I didn't ask the right questions and look at things closely enough. Then, sure enough, a kid pops up. You know, kids don't ask to come into the world. They are put into the world. Having a child is something I take very seriously.

While R.J.'s mother and I were together, all you can operate on is trust in one another. While I may have suspected something irregular about her lifestyle, I did not foresee what I finally discovered. I learned belatedly that

R.J.'s mother, Pamela Vasser, had been a convicted prostitute. According to the *Chicago Sun-Times,* she had pleaded guilty to an outstanding charge of prostitution in 2001. An affidavit also supported the fact that her teenage daughter, Taylia Vasser, telephoned me to say that R.J. had been left home alone on occasion while Pamela went out on escort dates.

R.J. is 7-years-old and a great kid and he deserves every opportunity I can help provide for him in this world. Given the way his mother was living at the time, I wanted to give my son a chance. In order to do that I had to get him away from her.

Five years later, in January of 2008, my attorney, Steven Lake, filed a legal motion in Chicago to gain custody of my then -2-year-old son, Richard Jr. It was our contention that his mother did not provide a safe environment. During the custody battle, I wanted to make sure my son-especially being a black kid-had a chance in life.

I was awarded full custody of R.J. on November 10, 2009. I am so happy to have a son and I am willing to do anything to sacrifice on his behalf. He is worth everything. He is very intuitive and curious about everything. As a former professional athlete, I obviously look at his hand-eye coordination, size, strength and speed. But I want to emphasize education. That's what I keep pushing; I am just trying to help shape and mold what he wants to be. He is doing well and I am so happy to have him in my life.

In 2006 as I was celebrating my 46th birthday I met the love of my life.

I was at Japonais Restaurant in Chicago celebrating with Michael Jordan and a few other guys. I noticed a beautiful woman across the room. I decided to take a strategic approach: I scanned her group to see if I knew anyone there, and after identifying a familiar face, I went over to say hello to my old friend, Haven Cockerham.

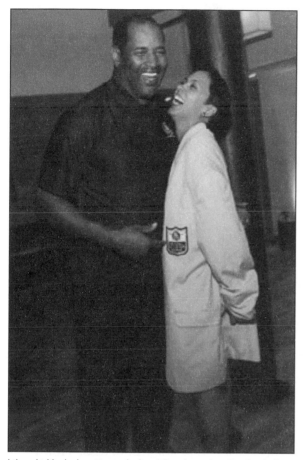

I thought I looked pretty good when I first donned my Pro Football Hall of Fame sports jacket during the week of my official induction. But I have to admit that my girlfriend, DeEtta Jones, looks much better wearing it. That entire week was full of laughs and strong emotions.

DeEtta and I recount the story now for friends and she swears that when I extended my hand and asked her name her mind went blank and she couldn't remember it. She loves to tell people that she loved me at first sight. I'll take that.

DeEtta and I dated from that point on for about a year. She lived in Washington, DC, and had a growing consulting practice, DeEtta Jones and Associates. Her business allowed her to come to Chicago regularly and we saw each other during those visits. She was professional and fun-loving, focused and spontaneous. She seemed to smile with her eyes when she talked. She made people feel good about themselves when she was around, never forgetting to say a kind word to people who served us in restaurants or carried our bags through airports. Her generosity of spirit spoke to me. I loved her early in our relationship, but she loved me more. That's what she always said back then. At the end of our visits in Chicago, as I drove her to O'Hare Airport, she would sit silently in the passenger seat clutching my right forearm as tears fell down her face. I think she was always afraid that each goodbye would be the last.

At that time, DeEtta had never been married and had no children. She is eleven years my junior and had focused almost solely on developing her career. When she talked to me about her wants I listened, but was not particularly interested in starting over with children. Also, I wasn't exactly emotionally forthcoming with her. She and I were dating just before my court battle to gain custody of R.J. began. I was a bit overwhelmed by all that I was learning about R.J.'s mom and preparing to do as a single dad – decisions that would change my life and lifestyle forever. My ability to fully invest in her just wasn't there. I also have to mention, we were in a long distance relationship and some would say I'm not the easiest person in the world to communicate with by phone. DeEtta likes to say that I'm a man of few words. That might be stoic and sexy when you get to see someone regularly, but trying to have a fulfilling phone-based relationship with someone like me was asking a lot.

In late summer 2007 she came to town on a business trip. Over dinner she told me that things weren't working out between the two of us, that she loved me more than I loved her and that's not enough to secure her ongoing investment. I asked her to be patient, that I was "going through something." After dinner we went for a long walk downtown, hand-in-hand like teenagers. We looked at the stars, sat on park benches and made water fountain wishes following her "wishing rules" – "wishes have to 1) be unselfish, focused on good for someone else, and 2) never told to a soul." I felt my heart open up a bit that night. We made love in the hotel room near her downtown office and the next morning I stood looking out the window as she walked to work. She called a month later to tell me that she had just married a man who loved her and wanted to have a family.

The news of DeEtta's marriage took a huge emotional toll on me. We didn't see or speak to each other for more than three years. A few times during those years I called and left voice messages; none of them were returned. Then one day, the day after my appearance at SuperBowl XLV in Dallas as one of the 2011 HOF inductees, she called. She congratulated me then without much other

Having my girlfriend, DeEtta Jones, and our son Shiloh, present at the Hall of Fame ceremony in Canton, Ohio, made that spectacular day even more special. Being able to share my good fortune with the ones I care the most about lets me know that I am appreciated and loved. And one day Shiloh will be old enough to appreciate the magnitude of that event.

conversation, told me that she was suspicious about her young son's paternity. I listened, "I was on birth control when you and I were together. I knew that you didn't want children and that I would never want to have a child outside of a marriage. Then, after we separated and before I got married, I took several pregnancy tests – even a blood test administered in my doctor's office. They were all negative. My new husband and I quickly abandoned birth control and actively tried to conceive. I never had reason to doubt Shiloh's paternity. Then yesterday I got three calls in a row from my mom and two of my sisters. They saw you on television and called me because of the resemblance between you and Shiloh. Richard, the timeline works but it just doesn't make sense."

After a long pause I said, "Well, we better get to the bottom of this. Not knowing is going to eat you up inside."

We agreed to go through with a paternity test without alerting her husband. She also confided in me that she was not happy in her marriage. As she described it, it just wasn't the right fit. She had been considering leaving the marriage for nearly a year when the issue of Shiloh's paternity surfaced. The paternity test results came back positive. DeEtta shared the news with her husband, turning a strained situation into an impossible one. When I heard the news I gave the only response I could, "Come on home, baby." A few months later, she packed two duffle bags, put Shiloh in the car, and drove from Washington, DC, to Chicago. They've been here since then.

I can't say the transition was easy. She went through a difficult divorce while dealing with intense work demands, trying to help Shiloh adjust to a new life and family, and find her own place in "my world." One of the things she told me she was most afraid of is getting lost in my celebrity, being invisible. She has been careful to plant her own seeds in Chicago, personally and professionally, and to stay closely connected to her family and friends in DC. Things are now easy between us – our energies match. We like and respect each other as people. We're both professionally ambitious, intellectually curious, and see our multidimensionality as assets to be leveraged. Sometimes she and I sit up all night long talking about ideas, aspirations, even art. (We can't talk about sports because it's a subject she knows almost nothing about – had never heard my name when we met!) I truly believe that the two of us are the perfect example of 1+1=3. Maybe the three in this equation is Shiloh.

When Mary and Sarah first heard the news about Shiloh being their little brother they told DeEtta, "God gave you Shiloh to bring the two of you back together." Shiloh is quite a kid. I remember talking on the phone to DeEtta as she was driving from Washington, DC, to Chicago. She told me that I'd like

Shiloh, that he's a "special kid." He had just turned three when we met. At first he was whiny and clung to his mom. Within six months his pre-school advanced him to a class for kids who were four years old. They said that his verbal and technology skills were beyond his years. As I think back, his whole world was turned upside down at the age of three and he managed to get through it and even excel. As happy as I am that DeEtta and I were able to reunite, I'm even more pleased that Shiloh came through what could have been a devastating experience as a whole and happy child. He brings sunshine to our home every day now, telling me about his future aspirations to be an astronaut and a rock star. I can see him being either, or both, or whatever he wants to be. And I'm so happy that all the pieces came together allowing me to be his dad and to love his mom, again.

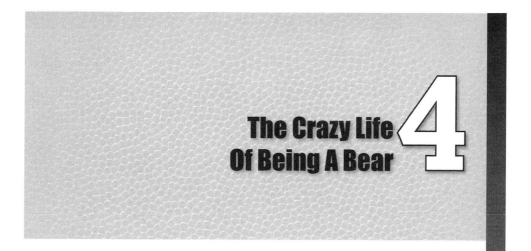

The Crazy Life Of Being A Bear 4

There were so many strange, hilarious, and sometimes shocking incidents that happened both on and off the field with the Chicago Bears in the 1980s. Many of those incidents were instigated by Walter Payton.

I vividly recall sitting next to Payton on a team flight during my rookie season. Walter said to me, " Hey, Richard, want to see me rip this deck of cards in half with my bare hands? How much do you want to bet me?"

I said, "Sure, I'll bet you whatever you want," figuring this was some sort of trick the veteran was going to play on the young player.

Walter grabbed the deck of 52 cards, placed his meaty hands around the cards and ripped the deck in half!

Amazing! But I questioned whether this was a trick deck of cards that he could tear easily. At that point, Walter yelled to one of the flight attendants, "Hey, Miss, can you get me another deck of cards?"

It took Walter a little longer to rip through the second deck, but sure enough, he did it. That's how strong and smart he was in using proper technique.

The thing about Walter is that you always had to keep your eyes peeled to see what he was up to. You knew that he was like a mischievous kid, always finding it hard to sit still and not cause some sort of reaction or disturbance.

He frequently set off cherry bombs or exploding cigarettes. He was notorious for that. A lot of the players smoked cigarettes during halftime in the locker room. I even remember once seeing Payton smoking in the locker room. I found that strange at the time.

Another curious thing that would happen off the football field was the treatment by veteran players of the rookies who did not fulfill their time-honored rookie obligations, such as getting donuts and milk in the morning for their veteran teammates on Saturdays.

If a rookie failed to come through with the donuts, the veterans would make him pay. Sometimes that meant taping the offending rookie to a goal post on the practice field. If this happened in November or December, it could be freezing out there, and if there was snow on the ground, the veterans would throw snowballs at the rookie who was tied to the goal post. The rookie would remain tied to the goal post until one of his buddies, another rookie, came to rescue him. You knew for certain that none of the veterans would untie the rookie.

Rookie hazing in the NFL is frowned upon now, and I suppose someone could get seriously injured if things got out of hand. But we managed to keep things under control back then, and it was all in good fun.

Back in the 1980s, we didn't have the sleek digital video equipment like they have now to capture game and practice footage. So the rookies were given the responsibility of lugging around the heavy cameras and other equipment to the team plane on Saturdays when we headed out for a road game. We would have eight road games plus possible playoff games on the road. So that meant a lot of lugging around, especially if you were the only rookie who made the team. You could be carrying that equipment yourself all year.

When I was a rookie in 1983, we also had Dave Duerson and Mike Richardson who were new to the defense. So we were able to take turns carrying the camera equipment to the plane. It was embarrassing to have to carry the equipment, because you were dressed nicely with a sport coat and tie. And sometimes the veterans would insist that the rookies bring chicken or some other favorite food on the plane for them. You never knew quite what to expect.

Another incident that sticks out in my memory was the sight of Payton driving down Illinois Interstate 90 toward O'Hare Airport. We both were a little late getting started toward the airport to catch the team flight and traffic must have been backed up a bit. I looked out my side-view mirror and saw that Walter had a police escort. Seeing that, I quickly decided to jump in behind him and take advantage of the opportunity to get to the airport more quickly. The police car had its lights flashing and we were able to easily weave our way through traffic. That's the kind of influence Payton had in the city of Chicago back then. That was quite the scene.

The only other Chicago sports person I can recall getting that type of special treatment was my friend, Michael Jordan. Sometimes when we were at his old restaurant in downtown Chicago on LaSalle Street late at night, playing poker, spades, or whatever ... if it was a snowy night or something, the cops would escort us all the way to Lake Street in the north suburbs. We appreciated the men and women who policed the Chicago streets. They respected us and we respected them, and we took care of them when it came to fundraiser appearances and events of that nature.

As Bears players, we were welcome to participate at the downtown gun club and even hold machine guns. That was quite an experience. One time we brought the great Bo Jackson with us, and he seemed to enjoy hanging out with us. Another time, someone near me was firing a gun so rapidly that one of the shells went down the back of my shirt. All I knew was that shell was hot! It was real scary that day.

Many other frenetic and unpredictable situations occurred with my Bears teammates during preseason games overseas. I remember when we went to London in 1986. A lot of us took taxi cabs to our destination, especially if we missed the team bus to practice sessions during the week before the game. One thing that really impressed me over there was that the cab drivers did not try to take advantage of their patrons. In other words, they were instructed to take the shortest and least expensive routes. We can't really say that about many cab drivers in the United States, especially when it comes to some of them taking advantage of out-of-towners.

The taxi service in London proved to be so reliable that many players preferred taking taxis instead of the team bus. Invariably, we would be hanging out late at night and having fun throughout the week. We knew we could sleep a little bit later the next morning and grab a cab to get us where we needed to go in plenty of time. Many times we would wind up getting to our practice site five or 10 minutes ahead of the bus. It was very convenient.

In 1988, we traveled to Sweden to play the Minnesota Vikings in a preseason game. The game was held at a large and famous soccer stadium in Gothenburg, Sweden. During the week leading up to the game, we practiced at another soccer stadium. As we were practicing one day, a Swedish model was posing for commercial pictures along the track that surrounded our practice field. Now, you have to remember that the people in Sweden are much more liberal about their bodies and sex in general than most Americans; you probably could say the same thing about most people who live in Europe.

Anyway, this model casually removed her sweater to change into another outfit in front of the cameraman. When she removed her sweater, she was not wearing anything underneath. Well, you can imagine what the reaction was like for about 50 red-blooded American football players. Coach Ditka nearly swallowed his whistle, and everybody kind of froze in disbelief on the field. When the young model realized that we were not accustomed to seeing such an outdoor show, she laughed and quickly covered up. Besides playing the game later that week, that model had to be the highlight of our trip to Sweden. Here we are practicing football, and she is taking her clothes off next to us. We were all wondering what piece of clothing was going to come off next. It was difficult to concentrate on football when something like that was going on just a few yards away.

When the actual game came around, the Vikings wound up winning the symbolic trophy. The Minnesota players were even drinking beer out of the trophy, as if they had just won the Super Bowl or something. Later that evening after the game, as members of the Bears and Vikings were partying together at a bar in the town of Gothenburg, my boisterous teammate Dan Hampton wanted to put a stop to the Minnesota players drinking out of the trophy, so he urinated into the trophy. We all got a laugh out of that. It was our way of saying that the Vikings, especially one of their linemen, Keith Millard, were not going to celebrate in front of us.

The fans in Sweden at that time weren't familiar with the rules of American football. In fact, the only time they seemed to get really excited was when a player kicked the ball: either an extra point, field goal, punt, or kickoff. I suppose that is because of their soccer orientation. That was the same case when we played in London in 1986. The other time the fans made a lot of noise in London was after a streaker came out on the field. Streaking was very popular in the 1980s all over the world, it seemed. Never a dull moment.

Even our assistant coaches were subject to some inadvertent abuse from players from time to time. Dale Haupt was the Bears defensive line coach from 1978-85. One time Dale was trying to help us warm up before a game. He was snapping the ball before the defensive linemen would charge forward. We always would sort of brush up against him, and of course he did not have the protection of a helmet and pads. One time one of us charged after the snap of the ball and hit him so hard that he got flipped over backwards and ended up with a big turf mark on the back of his head. We all kind of joked that he had it coming because he had been like a drill sergeant with us. Up, down, up, down! That's how Dale and Buddy Ryan started every practice session. We defensive players didn't like that, and we didn't like running the gassers, you know, running back and forth across the field.

So we made a bet with Buddy Ryan. We agreed that if we didn't lose a game in 1985, we weren t going to have to run those gassers. That was an incentive for us not to lose. The gassers were Ryan's way of getting us game-ready, so to speak. But we didn't think they were necessary, especially since Ditka was going to make us run sprints after practice. We didn't have to run like that until after we lost our only game, which was to Miami in Week 12.

Make no mistake about it, this contentious relationship between Ditka and Ryan had been brewing from the start, and everything finally boiled over during that Miami loss. There were a lot of brash personalities on the team and everyone was angling for personal gain through commercial endorsements and public appearances. And, of course, you had coaches like Ditka doing the same thing. It was like the Wild, Wild West. That's the way I looked at it. One day Coach Ditka is roller-skating through Halas Hall or calling people out through the press or grabbing his crotch along the sideline. He was creating all of that attention, even though he wasn't the one who had to go out and play in the games.

Obviously, I think Buddy Ryan wanted his piece of the action, too, when it came to public attention and recognition for a job well done. When it came down to that game against Miami, we figured the Dolphins would be the only team left on the schedule who could possibly keep us from going undefeated. We already had beaten Green Bay once that season, and we'd already beaten the Patriots. We didn't know we would see New England again in the Super Bowl. So we thought we might run the table in the regular season if we could get past Miami.

I recall that a bunch of us players wanted to go to Miami a few days before that November game in order to get used to the warm climate. The general routine is that teams arrive the day before a game, so the coaches thought we just wanted to go down there early to have fun and party. That wasn't the case at all. Sure, everybody likes to have a good time in a warm-weather city, but we actually were thinking more about finding a better way to prepare for a very important game.

I mean, when I am at home in Chicago, you can't tell me when my curfew is. So when we go on the road, don't tell me what my curfew is. We weren't college kids. We go to practice, do our thing, whatever.

When we played the 49ers in '84, we were allowed to hang out without a curfew in San Francisco. It was 4 or 5 in the morning and we realized we had to get back to the hotel. I remember spending $120 just to get a cab to take us back to the hotel near Santa Rosa, California where the team stayed.

When the taxi pulled into the hotel, one of the coaches was pulling into the place right in front of me; he had been out all night, too. So the point of it is that we all come to work and do our thing. In similar fashion, I wanted us to go to Miami a few days before the game. I thought it would be cool, but we didn't do it.

In the Dolphins game, Buddy Ryan had our defense blitzing quarterback Dan Marino. But Miami was the first team to really use their offensive set to spread us out defensively; they spread us out because they wanted to see the blitz coming. With that, they would have a hot read to get rid of the ball quickly when they spotted a blitz. Marino would roll out away from me, trying to get our outside linebacker Wilber Marshall out in the flat with a wide receiver. And they were posting our safety Gary Fencik up with their wide receiver Nat Moore, putting Fencik in a one-on-one situation. So they were attacking with Nat Moore. They felt that Gary was the weak link if they got him out in space. They wanted to force him to come up and make tackles, leaving him vulnerable to the pass by using that little half roll-out by Marino. Meanwhile, our offense wasn't very effective in the first half.

We all knew that Miami was last in the league in stopping the run, yet we were passing a lot in the first half. We didn't show patience by passing so much, even though we had the best running back in the game in Walter Payton. By the end of the game, Steve Fuller had completed 11 of 21 pass attempts and Jim McMahon had connected on 3 of 6.

Buddy got pissed off at Ditka at halftime because Ditka wanted him to stop ordering so many blitzes. Ryan's response was: "You stop throwing the ball and run it!" That's what got everybody pissed off. We had the No. 1 guy in rushing. The Dolphins shouldn't have even been on the same field with us. We should have been running, running, running to keep the ball away from Marino and their pass offense.

That was a constant theme all year. Ditka was always telling Buddy to stop blitzing so much. Buddy's reply always was: "Get some points on the board and maybe I can stop blitzing." That was the give-and-take the players always heard.

There also was friction between Ditka and Ryan because Ryan had been hired by George Halas before Ditka became head coach of the Bears. Ditka was hired basically to run the offense. If both sides had had the same personality, our team probably would not have had such a wild attitude. I think the players realized that Halas set it up that way.

Also keep in mind that our backup quarterback Steve Fuller started that Miami game; Jim McMahon came in after Fuller broke his foot. Despite that loss to Miami, Payton kept his record streak of 100-yard rushing games intact at 11. I believe McMahon changed some calls sent in by Ditka from the sidelines to make sure Walter got his 100 yards. Payton wound up with 121 rushing yards in that game.

We all know the game of football is not about personal goals. But I think a coach should be respectful. You mean to tell me that if Walter had been a quarterback and had never thrown a touchdown pass in the Super Bowl or another important game – or if he had a streak of games with touchdown passes – that he wouldn't have been given that opportunity? To me it's disrespectful when a coach says, "Oh, I didn't remember about the streak," or something like that. Come on, let's be real.

When Ryan and Ditka went at it during halftime, I didn't see anything, but I heard movement. Maybe there was a swing and people pulling them apart. But I kind of knew what was taking place because I saw what was happening on the sideline earlier.

The banter and cussing and fussing that was going on constantly between those two reminded me of what it was like for a kid growing up in a house where the parents are yelling and screaming and fighting with each other all the time. As a kid, you know what is going on. I grew up with that in my house. I knew what was happening. When you have been around abuse, you hear it, you feel it, but you carry on. You are aware of it. You just understand what is going on. Same thing as a player.

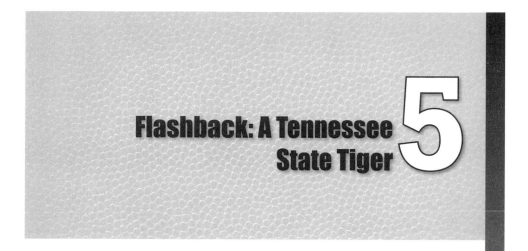

Flashback: A Tennessee State Tiger 5

I moved on from Murphy High School in Atlanta after playing just a year and a half of prep football, mostly as an offensive lineman.

Then came the very important decision of where to go to college. No one in my family had ever gone to college, so this was a big deal for me on many levels. I knew I was capable of playing football at the college level and applying myself academically. My overwhelming choice was to attend Tennessee State University, a historically black college in Nashville, Tennessee.

There is so much history and tradition with Tennessee State University. For me to be the first former Tiger to be selected to the Pro Football Hall of Fame in the 100-year history of the school is tremendously humbling and rewarding. I don't take that lightly.

Our coaches at Tennessee State were smart, creative, and innovative. I learned so much about the game and about trusting my teammates.

It was such a proud moment for me to have Joe Gilliam Sr. present me for induction to the Pro Football Hall of Fame, because he had a huge impact on my development as a player, and, ultimately,

Pressuring the quarterback was a skill that I honed at Tennessee State and later refined in the NFL. I give a lot of credit to my coaches at Tennessee State for teaching me to study the game strategically and exploit my God-given skills.

my life. He was born in Steubenville, Ohio, in 1923, which happens to be close to Canton, Ohio, home of the Pro Football Hall of Fame.

Gilliam began his college playing career at Indiana University. He wound up transferring from Indiana to West Virginia State University, where he became an All-American quarterback.

Gilliam later would become head football and basketball coach at Oliver High School in Winchester, Kentucky, from 1952 to 1954, and he won a state championship there in football in 1954.

The author of several books on football, Joe Gilliam, Sr. has been a respected football strategist for many decades.

From 1963-1981, the Tennessee State Tigers won seven Black National Championships.

Gilliam was picked as Coach of the Year in the Ohio Valley Conference in 1990, and later inducted into the TSU Sports Hall of Fame. His career record of 254-93-15 included coaching five undefeated teams and five other teams that lost only one game. Gilliam helped direct numerous players into pro football. He also has worked with the Arizona Cardinals' coaching staff as an offensive consultant during their training camp.

Gilliam, who has conducted summer football camps and clinics for underprivileged children in Nashville, Tennessee, has received numerous national and regional awards, including the All-American Football Foundation Lifetime Achievement Award and the College Football Hall of Fame Contribution Award.

The legendary John Merritt was the head coach at Tennessee State when I played there. Merritt and Gilliam had a long-time coaching relationship. In 1955, Gilliam joined Merritt's coaching staff at Jackson State University before leaving to become the head coach at Kentucky State in 1957.

Gilliam was defensive coordinator at Tennessee State from 1963 to 1983. While at Tennessee State I came to know him and really respect him and his football mind. Six years after I left Tennessee State to join the Bears Coach

Gilliam took over as head coach at Tennessee State in 1989 and held that position until 1992. Gilliam was named Ohio Valley Conference Coach of the Year at Tennessee State in 1990

Coach Merritt died on December 13, 1983, at the age of 57. Another bad coincidence on my birthday.

Coach Merritt led us to our school's first-ever Division 1-AA playoff victory in 1982, my senior season. His career record at Tennessee State was 174-35-7, and he was inducted into the College Football Hall of Fame in 1994. He has a street named after him in Nashville – John Merritt Boulevard, and Tennessee State opens every season playing against Alabama A&M in the John Merritt Classic.

When I consider the conditions I grew up in, there were not a lot of positive male role models for me to follow, so Coach Gilliam became one for me at Tennessee State. I just dreamed and tried to stay on track. I had a lot of older brothers who showed me a lot of things that I didn't want to do. From drugs to fighting to whatever, I had a first-hand look.

So coaches such as Gilliam and Merritt became quite influential during an important period of development for me.

Coach Gilliam's son, the late Joe Gilliam Jr., gained national acclaim as a superb college quarterback at Tennessee State and ultimately started ahead of Hall of Fame quarterback Terry Bradshaw with the Pittsburgh Steelers. In fact, Gilliam was a two-time All-American at Tennessee State. But the younger Gilliam, known as Jefferson Street Joe, would succumb to drug and alcohol issues that cut short his pro career. He reportedly had been sober for four years before dying of a heart attack at the age of 49 after watching a game between the Dallas Cowboys and Tennessee Titans on December 25, 2000.

No doubt, the demise of Joe Jr. had a huge impact on the entire family. He had been selected in the 11th round of the NFL draft in 1972 and actually started the first six games of the '74 season ahead of the more-celebrated Terry Bradshaw.

By 1975, young Joe Gilliam was out of the NFL. He tried to make a comeback by playing semi-pro football with the New Orleans Knights and in the upstart United States Football League, playing with the Washington Federals. But his cocaine addiction and alcohol problems got the better of him and he wound up living on the street for a period of time.

The impact Joe Gilliam Sr. had on my life has been immeasurable. As a pioneer in coaching, and as a proud black man who endured the racism of the '50s and '60s, he was amazing. Imagine a man with a master's degree having to work labor jobs to make a living before getting opportunities to coach.

Coach Gilliam gave me responsibilities and leadership opportunities at Tennessee State. I was the captain and called the signals for the defense. I appreciated the fact he trusted me and allowed me to fulfill those roles. I was very knowledgeable about the game, and I appreciate the game to this day.

In my speech for the Hall of Fame, I talked about Tennesse State's powerful influence on me. This is what I said, "I have so many people to thank and be thankful for when it comes to my Hall of Fame selection, including Coach Gilliam. I know my mother is jumping in Glory. I know that my high school coach William Lester, who just passed away in 2009, would be pleased. I had the privilege of sharing my experience of being inducted into the Georgia Sports Hall of Fame with him. And to be the first Pro Football Hall of Famer from a school that has existed for 100 years … I don't take that lightly. We know that the NFL adopted their pro offenses from the historically black colleges. If you had told me 10 or 20 years ago that I would become the first Hall of Famer from Tennessee State, I wouldn't have believed you. Because when I looked at a former Tiger like Claude Humphrey, a guy that I watched as a kid at Tennessee State, and Ed "Too Tall" Jones, who stood the test of time after being drafted first overall by the Dallas Cowboys in 1974, it is just hard to believe.

"My Hall of Fame honor really is the first cumulative award for my professional career. I always wanted to be named NFL Defensive Player of the Year or NFC Defensive Player of the Year, or at least Defensive Lineman of the year. When you lead the league in sacks two years in a row, you figure one of those is going to happen. Yes, I won the Super Bowl MVP trophy. But I never received an honor for an entire season or a career until this amazing Hall of Fame honor. And, baby, it just doesn't get any better than that."

"For a kid who came out of Murphy High School and didn't play but a year and a half of high school football … started as an offensive lineman and somehow got on defense … I am so grateful and so happy to be in this Hall of Fame class.

"Coach Merritt used to say that the "hay is in the barn" when he talked about the practice and work in preparation for a game. That's how I felt at the end of my NFL career while I awaited a call from the Hall of Fame. My work is done. I can't come back and do any more. My day has come.

"This is huge for me and my family and where I came from, it has been overwhelming. I couldn't imagine that I would get this kind of response."

So many great football players have worn the Tennessee State uniform over the years: Claude Humphrey, Ed "Too Tall" Jones, Noland Smith, Larry Kinnebrew, just to name some of the dozens and dozens of Tigers who made it to the NFL.

One of my teammates at Tennessee State was Steve Moore, who came into the NFL the same year I did and went on to play with the New England Patriots. It was ironic that we ended up playing *against* each other in Super Bowl XX in New Orleans.

I learned right away at Tennessee State that there were any number of players with great reputations in high school who had to prove themselves

Three of the greatest college football coaches of all-time were (L. to R.) Jake Gaither (Florida A&M), Eddie Robinson (Grambling) and John Merritt (Tennessee State). Coach Merritt led us to our school's first-ever Division 1-AA playoff victory my senior season. His career record at Tennessee State was 174-35-7, and he was inducted into the College Football Hall of Fame in 1994.

all over again at the college level. This became a test of physical conditioning, mental toughness, strong determination, and a willingness to learn new concepts.

In order to get on the playing field at Tennessee State, every player had to run a certain time in conditioning drills to prove that he had the physical and mental toughness to make it at that level. That meant reporting to summer camp in decent shape. Talk about pushing your body to the limit! There were times when I thought I couldn't make it, but somehow I did.

In high school I had been an All-State selection in football and All-City in basketball. I could have gone to Alcorn State in Mississippi to play basketball. But Tennessee State beckoned me. Plus, I had a lot of friends going to Tennessee State. That was a major influence. I remember growing up in Atlanta watching local sports heroes such as Claude Humphrey, Tommy Nobis, and Hank Aaron. After I learned that Claude Humphrey went to Tennessee State, I was even more encouraged to follow in his footsteps. Humphrey was a terrifically gifted and physical defensive end who played most of his career with the Atlanta Falcons before finishing up with the Philadelphia Eagles.

I played all four years at Tennessee State, from 1979-1982, earning All-America honors from '80 to '82. I was named Defensive Player of the Year by the Sheridan Broadcasting Network in 1982, I was also named Defensive Lineman of the year during my time at Tennessee State. I finished my college career with 39 sacks, including 14 in '82.

In 1993, I was humbled and honored to be selected to the Tennessee State Athletic Hall of Fame. That meant a lot to me and my family.

I not only learned about perfecting my football skills at Tennessee State, but I also learned about the importance of giving back and giving others the wonderful opportunity I had to go to college.

About 14 years ago, I started the Make a Dent Foundation. The primary objective of the foundation is to improve the lives of children. Over the years, we have donated thousands of dollars to worthwhile organizations such as The Illinois Literacy Foundation, Big Brothers and Big Sisters of Kentucky, Colin Powell's America's Promise, Angels on the Fairway, United Negro College Fund, the Better Boys Foundation, and an endowment at Columbia College Chicago for under privileged kids getting their degrees in sports management.

I am proud to say that I have been able to help a lot of youngsters who grew up under difficult circumstances as I did.

It is sad to recall that the NFL, for many decades before the 1960s, virtually ignored talented African-American football players from historically black colleges in the South such as Tennessee State. Sure, there were occasional black players from those schools who were given a chance at the pro level, players such as Roosevelt Brown, Dick "Night Train" Lane, Tank Younger, and others in the 1950s and 1960s. But the NFL was slow to the party, if you ask me. Schools such as Grambling, Morgan State, Alcorn State, Jackson State, and Tennessee State would eventually become major resources of NFL talent.

Sweetness

I was fortunate to join the Bears when Walter Payton already had established himself as one of the premier running backs of all-time in the NFL. Even though Walter played on the offensive side of the ball, I took great pride in trying to emulate the way he went about his business. His confidence, his style, his direct manner … those are all qualities anyone would want to have in the game of football. I also admired the way Walter gave back to the community and interacted with the fans and the general public.

Walter always was willing to sign an autograph, pose for a picture, or simply have a conversation with someone after practice or on the street. He related well to others and displayed the kind of people skills more athletes today should strive to show.

There are so many funny stories regarding Walter; he was such a prankster.

As I recall, in my second year with the Bears in 1984, there was one particularly hot, sticky summer night in Platteville, Wisconsin, during training camp.

Payton was looking for a way to entertain himself and his teammates.

So he tossed a firecracker inside the dormitory at 4 o'clock in the morning!

Yep, Walter was the ultimate prankster, the guy you had better keep an eye on or else you might become his next victim.

If he wasn't tossing firecrackers, Walter was sneaking up behind someone and pulling down their pants.

Winning Super Bowl XX made the Bears a national phenomenon. Popular late night host Jay Leno (L) brought his Tonight Show to Chicago for a week in 1998. Walter Payton (R) and I were participants in funny skits for the show. This was the last time I saw Walter alive.

He did that to Matt Suhey, our fullback, right in the middle of practice one day. He pulled his shorts down in front of everybody right before the offense was getting ready to run a play.

I will always remember Walter's kindness with kids. He was always playing catch with a kid in the crowd when he wasn't doing something in practice. And he would stay after practice and sign autographs for anyone who asked.

Another funny story I heard about Payton probably wasn't so funny to everybody else at the time.

Matt Suhey had a nice Rolex watch with diamonds on it and everything. Matt was in Walter's trailer in Platteville and happened to leave the watch there by accident. So Walter thought he would hide it for a week. Matt was very concerned that someone had stolen his expensive watch. In that five-day period until Walter gave the watch back, the director of the university where we had our training camp, Steve Zielke, must have interviewed 100 people who could have had access to it. That's all he did for five days. He couldn't sleep at night. Zielke was wondering who could have done this. He even said to himself: "The Bears are going to leave Platteville if I don't find that watch...."

Then, one day Walter comes up and says innocently: Matt, did you lose this watch?

Zielke was furious.

I was sorry to see the end of the 18-year relationship between the Bears and Platteville, a town of about 10,000, in 2002.

The memories and funny anecdotes associated with the long-time Bears summer training camp will never die. In fact, they undoubtedly will become embellished over time, now that the Bears have re-located to Olivet Nazarene University in Bourbonnais, Illinois.

In addition to being a fabulous football player, Walter was an even better human being. He was genuine and he loved people. He left us too soon at the age of 45 on November 1, 1999. Payton died of bile duct cancer, nine months after disclosing he had a rare liver disease.

Walter always had a way of bringing out the best in his teammates – the best performances, the best laughs, and the best inspiration.

It was that way during his Hall of Fame career, and oddly, that way again during his funeral. Virtually every member of the 1985 Super Bowl team alternately shed tears and shared hugs during a private memorial service at Life Changers International Church in Barrington Hills, Illinois.

Many dignitaries, including then-Illinois Governor George Ryan and Chicago Mayor Richard M. Daley were among the mourners at an invitation-only service. Then-NFL commissioner Paul Tagliabue, who later told reporters that the NFL's Man of the Year award would be named for Payton, joined relatives to pay final respects to the league's career rushing leader at the time.

Club owners Ed and Virginia McCaskey and team president Ted Phillips headed up the Bears entourage.

Walter's widow, Connie, and children, Jarrett and Brittney, were among family members who greeted friends during a visitation prior to the service. A huge portrait of Payton in his Bears uniform stood behind them. Payton's body was cremated and his ashes sat in an urn on the altar.

Pastor Gregory Dickow told mourners, "This is a celebration of Walter Payton's life. He made his greatest gain on Monday when he died. He gained heaven. This is a celebration because this man, Walter Payton, is with his Lord Jesus Christ."

Payton's son, Jarrett, then a freshman football player at the University of Miami, eulogized his father in an emotional tribute. Jarrett recalled how difficult it was for his father to communicate with him in public because so

Walter Payton, shown here with his son Jarrett during his Hall of Fame induction, was a tremendous inspiration to me. The way "Sweetness" handled himself on and off the field resonates with me, even to this day.
(Photo courtesy of Pro Football Hall of Fame)

many others tried to listen in on their conversations. From the time Jarrett was a young child, Payton would use a whistle in public to get his son's attention or to deliver a sign of encouragement.

When Jarrett played in his first college game against Boston College earlier that year, Payton was too ill to attend the game. But Jarrett told the congregation: "I swear I heard a whistle in the crowd, and I turned around and didn't see him. I will always remember that moment."

Jarrett went on to say: "Many of you knew my father as a football player or businessman. I knew him as dad. He was my hero. My mother, my sister and I will miss him ... but he is in a place where there is no sickness, no pain."

Succeeding Walter Payton was a tough act to follow, but Neal Anderson did a great job and is perhaps one of the most under-appreciated former Bears players. Payton spent a lot of time counseling young Bears players, even after he retired from playing the game. (Photo courtesy of Mike Kinyon)

Eddie Payton, Walter's brother, thanked the media for its graciousness in not going overboard in its disclosure of the terminal aspect of Payton's disease.

Eddie, who was a star football player in his own right at Jackson State before performing as a kick returner in the NFL, shared several humorous and sentimental stories about his famous brother. "My memory is a lot like my stature – short, but not bad," he said.

NFL sportscaster John Madden, now retired, called Payton the "greatest football player I have ever seen. He was the total package. There are three kinds of people: those who make things happen, those who watch things happen, and those who don't know what's happening. Walter made something happen."

Mike Singletary emphasized Payton's courage and unselfishness "and acceptance of the Lord," in his remarks. Singletary also urged the former Bears teammates not to wait for another sad occasion to stay in contact.

Walter Payton broke Jim Brown's all-time NFL career rushing record of 12,312 yards in a game against the New Orleans Saints at Soldier Field on Oct. 7,1984, and afterwards he conducted a press conference. He even received a congratulatory phone call from President Ronald Reagan. In his typical light-hearted manner, Payton wrapped up the call by telling the President: "Give my regards to Nancy." (Photo courtesy of Mike Kinyon)

Mike Ditka quoted scripture as his voiced cracked with emotion in describing Payton, the football player and the person.

"He was the best runner, blocker, teammate, and friend I have ever met," said Ditka. "I love Walter Payton. What is his legacy? It's the mark he leaves on all of us. That's better than scoring touchdowns. Walter was special. He was sweet."

Payton rushed for 16,726 yards during his Hall of Fame career. I am proud to be able to join him in Canton, Ohio, among the all-time greats.

"When you find a treasure, you hold onto it, you don't let it go and you don't forget it. Walter Payton was a treasure," said Madden.

More than 565,000 people have joined the Illinois Organ/Tissue Donor Registry since February 1999, when Payton announced he had a rare liver disease and needed a transplant. Since his death, more than 300,000 names have been added. There are now almost five million people on the Illinois registry, the largest in the nation. He did not die in vain.

Rushing the Quarterback 7

One of the criticisms I heard throughout my career that irks me to this day was that I did not give 100 percent all the time, that I took plays off. That could not be further from the truth, and I take great offense to that characterization.

Fact is, I worked diligently before, during, and after the football season to make sure I was in the best possible condition to not only handle the rigors of playing in the National Football League, but also to excel as I did.

What people don't understand is that when they say I am taking plays off ... well, you stand in front of me on the field and see if you think I am taking plays off. Is a baseball pitcher taking plays off when he throws three balls and one strike? You call that taking off? You know that the pitcher has a great fastball and a great curveball, but because he doesn't throw it, do you say he is not giving his best effort? No, of course not.

What do most people generally say in that instance? They say that the pitcher is toying with the batter, trying to set him up for his best pitch. He is not giving the batter a good pitch to hit. OK, listen: pass-rushing in football is the same thing, the same mindset. I couldn't care less what the critics might be thinking, until they get in front of me. Then you will see what taking off really feels like.

My point is that the critics are not in my head and don't know football. For instance, if I am playing in the AFC compared to the NFC, I know that the AFC is dominated by pass-rushers because AFC teams throw the ball more. In the NFC, especially where the Bears play in the Midwest, it used to be predominantly a running conference. Why? Because of the climate in those cities.

I understood the parameters within which I was working. We played in a lot of low-scoring, defensive battles, and opposing coaches tried not to subject their quarterbacks to situations where they could be abused by strong defenses like ours. It was more difficult for me to produce big sack numbers against teams in our old NFC Central (now the NFC North) because those teams respected and understood what was taking place.

A successful defense thrives on the entire unit having an awareness and hunger to get to the ballcarrier or the quarterback. In this instance, former Bears defensive lineman Tim Ryan hits the quarterback low as I hit him high. (Photo Courtesy of AP Images)

Defensively, we tried not to be too predictable. If you rush the quarterback at 100 miles an hour every play, you will be susceptible to getting trapped or having a screen pass thrown in your direction after you have been sucked into the backfield. In addition, running up and down the field every play will get you worn down, just like a car. That man-made car runs out of gas. An overly-aggressive football player will run out of energy if he doesn't pick his spots judiciously.

My philosophy regarding pass-rushing was: Why show an opposing player your best stuff all the time? If I continue to show you my best stuff, eventually you are going to get the timing, figure out what is coming and know how to deal with it. I don't need to show you my best stuff throughout the game. You cannot beat me with my best stuff. All I need to do is exploit your weaknesses. I have to figure out your tendencies as an offensive lineman. How do you come out of your stance? What's your first move? How do you tip off what the play is going to be?

Another factor that my critics don't account for is how I was able to deal with double-team blocks from the tight end or a guard or whomever. Some guys such as Chris Hinton used to retreat quickly into the backfield to set up his block. I had to try to make him slow those steps down because I knew I could beat him inside to get to the quarterback. Each blocker has different footwork that I had to figure out before committing.

Once again, I knew that I could not give the opposition my big play move all the time. It wasn't a matter of taking plays off. I had to make sure I was setting up the defense for the right time to display my best moves. It would not be smart to display my best move early in the game. People who were using the criticism of me that I was not giving my best effort all of the time were not working with a full deck. But I am giving those critics the full deck now. You have to know what's in those 52 cards, so to speak. Otherwise, you re-adjust out there. People just don't know. I treated pass-rushing just like a pitcher approaches a batter. It's like the change-up that a pitcher uses to keep a batter off balance. That is what I tried to do so that the blocker could not know exactly what to expect from me in the way of a pass rush. I had to try to mess with his timing.

My objective always was to make life miserable for the offensive players. I wanted to make them uncomfortable to the point they did not want to come into contact with me. I wanted them to dread the task and shy away from it. I wanted them to know that my space was my territory only. I wanted to make a statement of some sort with every play. I believed in dictating what was going to happen on my side of the ball.

From the time I was in college, I worked out quite a bit. We trained as a team, even during the school year, twice a day. We were not allowed to take any classes that started after 1 p.m. because we had to be on the playing field by 3 p.m. on Monday, Tuesday, and Wednesday. Then we would have dinner about 4:45 p.m. and get back on the field by about 6:30 p.m. for another hour or hour and a half. Then it was back to our rooms for study time. That was the college regimen.

I was stronger than most people realized in college, even though I wasn't a fanatic about weight-lifting. I could do the military press over my head with about 310 pounds; I could bench press over 400 pounds; I could do the clean-and-jerk maneuver with about 340 pounds. With the leg press, I was pretty strong with that. Can't remember what my maximum was with it.

A major part of conditioning at Tennessee State was running two miles around the track in less than 14 minutes, 45 seconds. Then the next day we had to run the mile in six minutes in the morning. And we would run the quarter mile in the afternoon under 60 seconds. The next morning we would run four sets of 220s. The first one had to be under 27 seconds. Then we had about 80 seconds to get back to the starting spot again. The next one had to be under 29 seconds, then 30 seconds and, finally, 31. We were allowed to miss only one of those benchmarks, and you could not miss the last one.

Then we would hit the football field. That was kind of strenuous. After I got to the NFL, the burden to be at the top of your game physically was really up to the individual. How dedicated are you? Can you beat your competition? Can you outlast your opponent in the fourth quarter because of your conditioning?

Sure, we had people to oversee us and push us and direct us. If you sloughed off and didn't take the personal responsibility to be in top shape, you would only be hurting yourself and jeopardize being a member of the team.

I believed in dictating what happened on the playing field, forcing the opposing offense to feel uncomfortable and limited in what they could possibly execute. When we succeeded in doing that, often a sack such as this one I am applying to the Redskins' Joe Theismann was the result. (Photo courtesy of Mike Kinyon)

Usually, it was our position coaches who would push us to run sprints or laps. Or we would take it upon ourselves during the off-season to run hills or run stadium steps, whatever it took. We all knew that if you didn't take care of your body and work as hard as you could to maximize your ability on the playing field, well, your opponent would be able to overtake you. The level of skill and physical ability at the professional level is so high that better conditioning could be the difference between winning and losing. All of us felt like we were in a street fight with our opponents every time we met on the field. But how long can you last? How long can you compete? If you are not in good shape, it is going to be a quick fight.

In the fourth quarter of games, if I was tired, I knew that the guy in front of me was tired. That is what pushed me to do a little bit more in practice. It was a matter of working out for a living back then. I continue to work out now, but the motivation is quite a bit different. Back when I was competing in the NFL, I felt the need to push my body to the utmost extent.

When I was in the NFL, after the season ended, I used to go to Europe for the whole month of March and hang out in a time share I had over there. I would do a little cardio work, maybe jog or walk a bit, just to keep something going. But I basically would take that month off to let my body heal from a grueling NFL season.

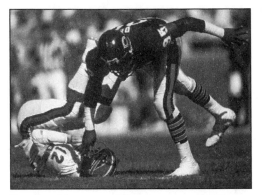

There is nothing more satisfying to a pass-rusher like me than getting to the quarterback and forcing him to get rid of the ball quicker than he wants, or actually getting a sack. Here I am, paying a visit to former Buffalo Bills quarterback Jim Kelly. (Photo courtesy of Mike Kinyon)

By April, I would start jogging again, riding bikes, and running stadium steps. I felt that if I went after an activity for about 45 minutes as hard as I could go after it, the routine was fine and beneficial. That would at least handle the cardio side of exercise. Then, by the latter part of April, I would start lifting weights and carry that into May, on Mondays, Wednesdays, and Fridays. I would do some kind of cardio activity on those days, as well. On those Tuesdays, Thursdays, and Saturdays, I would do straight cardio work to get the heart pumping. It might include running in the pool or riding horses.

A lot of people are not aware of the benefits of riding horses. I rode horses a lot in the NW suburbs of Chicago and in Georgia; I love horses. I found that riding horses was very good for strengthening my groin muscles and my hamstrings. Because of that, I never really had any groin injuries while playing football. I was amazed at how much you have to use your legs while riding a horse. I did have hamstring issues here and there, but that was not a major problem for me after my rookie year with the Bears.

I owe a great deal of gratitude to Bob Scholtz, who helped rehabilitate me when I had issues with my knees during my playing career. Bob, who had a performance training facility in Highland Park, Illinois, helped a lot of Bears players to remain on the field.

One of the superstitions that players on the Bears used to have was that if you sat on the team airplane next to Walter Payton, you would wind up getting hurt on the football field. Seemed kind of silly to me at first, but that is what happened to me. I got hurt during my rookie year, after sitting next to Walter on a team flight.

By June, I would start doing two workouts a day. In the second workout, I would work on agility drills, jumping back and forth across benches, trying to maintain body control. Balance and leverage were my strong suit. The speed I had was great, but if you can't leverage yourself and you can't balance it, then it is just plain speed. I often would get into awkward positions, but it is leverage and balance that are most important when you get into that position. If the groin and hip strength are not there, you can lose your balance. I believe that when the smallest muscles are firing, they are firing to the major muscles, but when that small muscle is not firing, that major muscle will collapse at some point and the joint will collapse. The small muscle has to fire. It's like a piston.

If you work the abdominal muscles and the hip flexors, that's where you get stronger and get leverage. That is where all the power and the strength come from: the hip flexors and the abs. The whole body fascinates me, and I knew as a football player you had to condition it like a missile. You have to make it all strong. When I trained, that was my mission.

During my training, not only would I run up hills, but I would also back-pedal up a hill. That would help my quadriceps muscles. That made my stride even stronger. If I wanted to work on speed, I would just run down the hill and still try to keep my body under control.

That kind of training and conditioning gave me the confidence to run down a ballcarrier or the quarterback when I was lined up on the backside of a play.

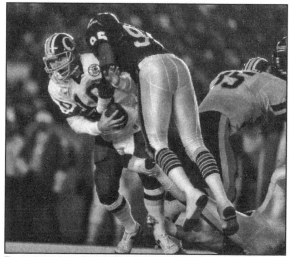

There were times during my career when I was not afraid to launch my body toward a quarterback or running back. I always felt as if I was in control of my body, even while I was in the air. Here I turn into a guided missile to take down the Redskins' Jay Schroeder.
(Photo courtesy of Mike Kinyon)

Clyde Emrich was one of the NFL's first strength coaches, and he has worked with many Bears' players during his 40 years with the organization.

I was proud to be known by Emrich as one of the strongest Bears players he ever worked with during his career.

Emrich, who was an Olympic weightlifter, always mentions a number of other exceptionally strong former Bears from various eras, including Walter Payton, Doug Atkins, Stan Jones, Bobby Douglass, Dan Hampton, Steve McMichael, Mike Hartenstine, William Perry, Doug Plank, and Trace Armstrong.

I owe a great deal to former Bears left tackle Jim Covert, who provided the greatest test of my ability during the many up-tempo practice sessions we had in training camp and during the season. I knew that if I could perform well against Jimbo, I could handle any of the other great offensive tackles in the league. Covert is a member of the College Football Hall of Fame and he was named to the NFL All-Decade Team of the '80s.

Among the more recent Bears' players, Emrich points out Tommie Harris, Olin Kreutz, Roberto Garza, Julius Peppers, Brian Urlacher, Lance Briggs, and Chris Williams.

One of my other former teammates who was always in top overall condition was wide receiver Willie Gault. Even to this day, Willie remains in great shape.

Willie is the one who really orchestrated the The Super Bowl Shuffle™ video for us. The famous line that he rapped started out: "This is Speedy Willie, and I'm world class."

He wasn't afraid to take chances and try new things on or off the field. I remember he performed the male lead with the Chicago City Ballet in 1986 to help raise money for a benefit.

As a wide receiver, Willie averaged 19.8 yards a catch during his five seasons (1983-87) with the Bears. With his world-class speed, he was able to spread defenses that always had to be aware of his downfield threat.

In addition to his extraordinary skills as a football player and track athlete at the University of Tennessee, Willie launched an acting career when his playing days were over.

Willie always has talked about the similarities between football and acting. Both take a great deal of commitment and dedication. Sure, football is more physical, with a lot of tiresome repetition in practice. He says that in acting there is more mental work where sometimes you have to be someone you are not. I guess you are pulling from all different areas of your life to become another character.

It's a shame Willie could not have been a part of the Bears after the 1987 season. The Bears decided not to offer him the type of money he deserved, and Willie signed with the Oakland Raiders.

There is always a lot of hand-fighting that goes on between offensive and defensive linemen. Here I am battling with San Francisco tackle Steve Wallace, a fellow native of Georgia. Controlling the lineman in front of you is key to success in the NFL. (Photo courtesy of Mike Kinyon)

When the Bears won the Super Bowl, we were one of the youngest teams ever to win it. The general feeling around the league was that we would be a dynasty and go on to win two or three more Super Bowls. But we played with the cards we had been dealt. We wish we had won three or four Super Bowls, but we didn't. A lot of great players play in this league a long time and don't win even one Super Bowl. Hall of Fame quarterback Dan Marino, of course, comes to mind. So I guess we have to be satisfied with what we were able to accomplish.

Times have changed in the NFL in terms of the expectations of teams. Players are expected to report to summer training camp in top condition and ready to go. Players are paid to attend off-season training sessions at their team's facilities.

When I think about my former Bears teammate William Perry, I recall a gifted athlete who defied physical logic in that era by being both a mobile and agile 350-pounder. We worked well together as I got to know him better because I had been in the league a couple of years before he came to the Bears as a rookie in 1985. I convinced William that I could take care of business when the runner went outside of the tackle position. When we worked together, we made the game easier because we knew where 80 percent of the plays were going to go.

The opposing offense couldn't get outside of me and they couldn't get through William. We knew we were going to have the opposition out-numbered; we knew we were going to have a linebacker free and unblocked in our area. We were able to dictate which way the offense was going to try to go.

So much was made about Fridge's weight in the media. I think I can remember William joining us in a pre-game meal twice. I think he was shy about that; I don't know what his issue was back then. Maybe he felt conspicuous and that other people were watching him when he ate or something of that nature. I remember one game we played in Green Bay and Fridge – instead of eating the pre-game meal with the team – had the ball-boy go and get him two or three brats before the game at Lambeau Field.

I wondered at the time about his decision to eat like that right before the game, but he went out on the field and showed me he could play at top form and deliver for the team. We never had a problem and we were able to talk to each other on and off the field.

William is a guy that I really appreciated and I know that he played the game the right way. When Mike Ditka decided to use Fridge as a goal-line running back, I don't think Ditka realized how big a story that would become on a national basis. His story really blew up and he became very popular. I don't think there was any jealousy within the team regarding Fridge because he was helping us win in so many ways. However there was some jealousy regarding his notoriety.

One unfortunate incident involving William Perry that will forever stick in my mind occurred in 1989 when we lost a controversial game to the Green Bay Packers by the score of 14-13. The game was later dubbed the "Instant Replay Game."

Packers quarterback Don Majkowski threw a game-winning touchdown pass to Sterling Sharpe with only a few seconds left to play.

At first, the play was called a touchdown. However, line judge Jim Quirk called a penalty on Majkowski for being beyond the line of scrimmage when he threw the pass.

Ultimately, the instant replay official ruled the throw was indeed legal and the Packers won.

When Majkowski made that pass across the line of scrimmage there was a lot of confusion and arguing on the field.

One of the officials yelled at Fridge and said: "Get back in the huddle, you fat-ass nigger!"

I went after the official and William grabbed me in the back of my shoulder pads to hold me back. After the game, we were so devastated about the loss that we couldn't really focus full attention on that ugly incident. I really should have done something right after that game.

There are a couple of things that have happened in my life that I wish I could live over again, and that was one of them. The other thing I would have done differently is that I would have spoken at my mother's funeral, even though I was overwhelmed with grief and emotion at the time.

I can't live that down as far as what happened to William Perry in Green Bay. I can't let that go in my life. There is never a place for anything like that.

For William to be in such poor health today is pretty scary. He is such a lovable guy with a big heart. He cares for people and I love him like a brother.

Out of the Mouths of Bears 8

I was blessed to have the opportunity to play alongside some incredible teammates with the Chicago Bears, with whom I shared so many memorable moments. In the spirit of objectivity, in this chapter I will let them have their say about our experiences and my unique circumstances. I'll do the same.

STEVE McMICHAEL

One of the most respected and dependable players in Chicago Bears history, Steve McMichael, was an integral part of our defensive units throughout the 1980s and early 90s. Mongo, as we all called him, was elected to the College Football Hall of Fame in 2010 because of his stellar career at the University of Texas.

Drafted by the New England Patriots in 1980, McMichael signed with the Bears as a free agent in 1981. One of the big reasons we were able to capture a Super Bowl title following the 1985 season was Steve

One of the most underrated players from our '85 Bears team was defensive tackle Steve "Mongo" McMichael. He was inducted into the College Football Hall of Fame in 2010, and he was a major reason that our Bears defense played with such a swagger.

McMichael. He had a streak of 101 games started until 1990, before his playing time was reduced. Mongo led the Bears with 11.5 sacks in 1988 and had 108 tackles in 1989. A two-time Pro Bowl performer, McMichael played for the rival Packers in 1994 before retiring. He later joked that he delighted in stealing money from the Packers organization by accepting a nice contract at the end of his career.

He wound up his pro career with 838 tackles, 95 assists and two interceptions.

Mongo always has been blunt about his feelings, almost to a fault. And he always has been a character who remains uncensored. Following his stellar pro football career, McMichael dabbled in pro-wrestling.

He wrestled two football players in 1997, beating Reggie White at Slamboree on May 18, 1997, before losing to Kevin Greene at the Great American Bash on June 15, 1997. By 1999, McMichael gave up pro-wrestling. He has been the successful head coach of the Chicago Slaughter of the Indoor Football League.

To give you an idea of how daring Mongo was even as a child, I remember hearing the story about what he did as a 4-year-old. He put a ladder on the side of a house, got on top of the house, and jumped while holding an umbrella, thinking he might be able to fly. It was probably a scene he had watched on a cartoon or something. He hit the ground a little faster than he had planned, unfortunately.

As a child, Steve lived in Pasadena, Texas, just south of the Houston Astrodome. In fact, the Astrodome was just being built about that time, and that's when young Steve first gained an understanding of the importance of football, especially in the state of Texas.

As fate would have it, Steve wound up playing in a high school all-star football game in the Astrodome. Then, while playing for the University of Texas, he played in the Astrodome again against the Houston Cougars. In the NFL with the Bears, we all played against the Oilers in the Astrodome, as well.

Steve was one of the few guys in the history of high school sports to make all-state three ways. One of those was as a kicker. He also ran the ball in high school and played on the line. A lot of people don't know that Steve once kicked a 48-yard field goal in college. Because of his strong leg and ability to kick off, McMichael was the backup kicker to Kevin Butler with the Bears.

If you ask Steve what made him most proud about his 13-year career with the Chicago Bears, he always gives the same answer: that he never missed playing in a game. That was 191 consecutive contests. That was the franchise record until 2010, when Bears long-snapper Pat Mannelly surpassed that mark.

As Mongo always says: "You're going to look in the mirror one of these days and you aren't going to like the person you see in it if you didn't give it all you had during your career."

IN STEVE McMICHAEL'S WORDS

Richard Dent is a true friend who paid attention to us veterans on and off the field, even when we didn't realize it. Mike Singletary and I used to sit around and talk about the Bible. I didn't realize until years after we all retired that Richard was listening in on those conversations in the locker room. And we also had those conversations during the flights to the away games.

Similar to my situation at the start of my NFL career, there is something to be said about those guys who come into the league with a chip on their shoulder. I had been drafted in the third round by the New England Patriots in 1980, but they cut me in training camp and said they thought I was part of a criminal element in the league. I had been hanging out partying and having a good time. Word got back to Patriots management, and they didn't like that much. It was a humbling experience.

By the time I got to the Bears as a free agent, I knew I had to prove myself all over again, prove that I could play in this league, and play well. There are a lot of guys who can play just as well as the more heralded guys, but for one reason or another, they need to refine their game, and have the opportunity to shine. That makes them seem like over-achievers, and those guys make great football players.

New England told me I wasn't good enough to start in this league, baby. But George Halas – "Papa Bear" – who signed me to my first contract, he was just mean enough to like who I was. As far as Richard Dent was concerned, we knew that the Colonel was going to be there doing his thing, come rain or shine. There is a reason folks nicknamed Richard 'The Colonel.' Back in the '80s there was a popular TV commercial for Colonel Sanders Chicken. It said that there was one thing he could do right like no other. That slogan applied to Richard when it came to sacking the quarterback. And I am sure he looked at me the same way. Very dependable. We took charge of the line of scrimmage. It's too bad that the kids playing in the NFL today are not more like that. They need more extroverts in the league today who are passionate about the game.

I think one of the reasons Richard didn't receive the kind of love he deserved early in his career was the fact that there were a lot of other great defensive ends in the league. You had Lawrence Taylor with the Giants, Reggie White with the Eagles and Packers, and Bruce Smith with the Buffalo Bills, just to name a few. All of them are Hall of Famers. They were all first-round draft picks out of college, who the fans and media were going to lavish a lot of attention and praise upon. Not so much on the 6th- or 8th-rounder, even though Richard was making the same plays.

What really impressed me so much about Richard was his versatility and ability to adapt. You could put Richard in any defensive scheme you want, and on any team you want, and he would make the same plays from the defensive end position. That's a Hall of Famer for you.

That's why the NFL pays the left offensive tackles so much money. The right defensive ends such as Richard Dent could make life miserable for those tackles.

Receiving Hall of Fame honors at this stage of our lives is significant. When I was named to the College Football Hall of Fame in South Bend, Indiana, in 2010, it only disappointed me that I did not have enough time to stand up there during my speech and thank everyone in my life who had something to do with that honor. Those kinds of awards are for the people who helped you along the way. That's why every Hall of Fame speech should be filled with thanks to each and every person who played a role in helping you reach that goal.

As a member of the Bears, we all were quite aware of the tension that brewed between Mike Ditka and Richard Dent. It seemed to fuel the competitive fire in Richard. I didn't mind having a guy who had something he was pissed off about coming out and venting on the football field. It wasn't just Richard who was able to do that.

Richard had so many special skills that separated him from the average football player. When he came off the snap of the ball, those first two steps, he was already up the field a yard farther than most guys. And that's what got him around that edge. His explosive first couple steps and quickness were unbelievable. Some guys are just fast. And some guys are fast and quick. That was Richard.

As far as I am concerned, this is the bottom line regarding Richard Dent finally getting into the Hall of Fame: It's about damn time. It was a sin not having him in there before now ... all of the plays he made, for God's sake.

DAN HAMPTON

Dan Hampton is a Hall of Fame defensive lineman who was a first-round draft pick of the Bears in 1979 out of Arkansas. We called him Danimal because he performed like an animal out on the field, creating problems for opposing offenses as a defensive tackle or end.

Hampton showed tremendous courage throughout his playing career, undergoing about a dozen knee surgeries. He recorded 82 quarterback sacks and was an incredibly disruptive force for our defense. When he was injured and missed games, our team felt his absence.

From 1983-90, in games Hampton missed, we only won 33 percent of the time. In games he played, we won 75 percent of the time. When he was

As a defensive unit on and off the field, we bonded and knew how to enjoy each other's company. At this 1994 golf outing, (L. to R.) William Perry, Steve McMichael, Tyrone Keys, Dan Hampton and I represent the Bears during an enjoyable charity event.

in the lineup, we sacked the quarterback 3.6 times a game and only 2.3 times a game without him. When Hampton played, we allowed an average of 14 points a game and allowed 23 points a game in the games he missed.

So Hampton's value to our team was very quantifiable.

Our defensive unit was filled with outstanding individual performers, but we thrived when we were healthy and together as a group on the field.

IN DAN HAMPTON'S WORDS

When Richard was drafted by the Bears in 1983, there was immediate talk that he couldn't gain weight because of some needed dental work. But, I remembered that when I first came out of college in 1979, I was skinny because they ran the hell out of us and we couldn't gain weight. So I realized that gaining weight wasn't going to be a big problem for Richard. After a couple of weeks in training camp, we all sort of realized that Richard and Mark Bortz were both low-round draft picks who would wind up making it as starters with the Bears.

Now, Richard did some things early on in training camp that were right and that secured him a spot on the roster. But the way Richard went about his business was completely different than what Bortz did. Mark Bortz was one of those fanatic-types who would do anything a coach asked him to do. If the coach asked him to run through a wall, Bortz would do it. Richard would run the drills, but you could tell that he wasn't gung-ho and concerned about what the coaches were thinking about his efforts in those drills.

After a couple of weeks, Buddy Ryan would always ask me what I thought about the kids, and I would say: "This Bortz kid, how could you not love him? He busts his ass all of the time, but he is not going to make our roster as a defensive tackle. He is not going to beat out Jim Osborne, Steve McMichael and me." So they moved Bortz to offensive guard, and that's how that happened. Then Ryan asked me: "What about the Tennessee State kid?"

I said, "He's the laziest son-of-a-bitch that I ever went to camp with." You know, when the offense is out there in practice, you are supposed to take four or five plays on defense and then let somebody else go in. You are supposed to rotate. You would have to send Richard an engraved letter to get his ass out there. He would be on the sideline hiding; he didn't want to do it, that kind of deal. I said, "He's lazy."

And then Buddy said something that was so profound. He said, "Yeah, but he always makes the right decision." To the normal person, you think he selects the low-calorie lunch when he has enough. No, Richard had awareness. Some people used to call it savvy. But as a defensive lineman, a great deal of the position is just awareness. Of course, size and speed are very important, as well. The kid the Bears had playing nose tackle in 2010, Anthony Adams, he has awareness. He doesn't look like a million dollars, but he knows how to play. And Richard Dent had that. Some people have that sixth sense.

Buddy Ryan noticed that any time the opposing offense ran that long trap play on him, Richard would close it. And if they ran it up the gut, Richard would bounce it. As a defensive lineman, you have to be able to recognize it within a split second to know what is coming. And Richard knew it. Most guys take several years to be able to recognize plays coming at them, but not Richard. All of those decisions came naturally to Richard. He was a complete player by the time he was 6-5 and 270 pounds. With him and me on the other end, we caused some headaches for folks.

I was more of a wrecker, and Richard was a catcher. You have got to have those different styles of play, because if everybody is a wrecker, who is going to catch the guy? And if you are the catcher, nobody is going to flush the quarterback, so you need both kinds of defenders. Richard was picture perfect for our defense as a guy with his height and great quickness and savvy. He was a force as a pass-rusher, but he wasn't going to go inside and let the quarterback get outside and cripple the defense ten times a game.

Richard was prototypical as a defensive end who could rush the quarterback. There were future Hall of Famers in Lawrence Taylor and Rickey

Jackson, but you couldn't stand them inside against an offensive tackle against the run. Richard Dent had the ability to rush the passer like Taylor and Jackson, but he also had the ability to post up a tackle and anchor the line of scrimmage.

Buddy Ryan would always tell us: "You dumbasses are going to have to be able to play the run and stop the run in order to be able to rush the passer." When I was in college at Arkansas, rushing the passer was no big deal because other teams ran the ball 70 times and passed 10 times. Big deal. In the pros, it didn't take us long to figure out that rushing the passer, that's where the money was and that's where the glamour was. But if the teams are running the ball five yards a clip, they aren't going to pass it. They don't have to pass it. So we knew we had to stop the run with the Bears. Richard was a fine player against the run. It just so happens that he was exceptional in the other parts of the game.

In the way of an unusual comparison, I look at what Charles Barkley was able to do on the basketball court. When you look at Barkley's round body, you wouldn't think he would have been able to accomplish the things he did as a Hall of Fame player in the National Basketball Association. How was he able to routinely score 30 points and grab 10 or 15 rebounds a game?

Richard Dent had that uncanny ability to swoop around the corner of the tackle in front of him, make a move and get right past him. He could swat the ball away or club the quarterback in the head. It doesn't take too many plays like that before the rest of the league takes notice. He became a special player that other teams had to account for when they game-planned for the Bears.

Our great middle linebacker Mike Singletary is in the Hall of Fame, and I don't think he had a touchdown in his career. I played 12 years and I never scored a touchdown. Richard scored two touchdowns and recorded a safety.

He knew where to be, he could read the schematics, and he knew where the blocking was trying to position us. He was a hell of a player, and he had a mean streak. One of the things I loved about him was that half the time I had to try to keep him out of a tussle on the field. The refs would say, "Hey, Hamp, get him back in the huddle."

All of us had a mean streak. We wanted to get you on the gravel and skin you up a little bit. There is nothing better than going to war with guys who love to go to war. That was the greatest part. Every Sunday at noon, it was time to go to war. It was sheer joy

As far as Richard's relationship with Mike Ditka, there was a lot of stuff going on behind the scenes, dating back to the drug test the Bears ordered Richard to take early in his NFL career. That's when the bad blood started. Now, did Ditka handle it the right way? I don't think so. Now, a lot of guys can't deal with success. I might be one of them. If you complimented me a whole lot, there is a part of me that relaxed a little bit. I was better as a guy that you basically taunted and said: "They told me you were a great player, and I don't think so." Richard Dent is the same way. And I don't think the Bears ever gave him his due respect. But, due to the fact that there was some bad blood in other areas and other issues, I don't think Richard ever saw through that and realized that maybe this was a coaching technique. When Ditka would call him Robert Dent, there was no question that it motivated him, and there is no question Richard played some of his best, hellacious football after that.

Was that the best way of motivating, say, Mike Singletary? Probably not. But I think that was sort of the trap that was laid for Richard, and once it was out there, they couldn't take it back.

One interesting thing I noticed was the fact that Bears president Ted Phillips expressed in the media that he regretted the fact the Hall of Fame game between the Bears and St. Louis Rams in Canton, Ohio, had been canceled due to the late consensus on the collective bargaining agreement. Phillips said that he wished more Bears fans would have been in Canton to celebrate the induction of Dent into the Hall of Fame the night before that game. I realized after reading Phillips's comments that finally they are according him a little respect.

When I went into the Hall of Fame, the Bears management didn't even come. I hate to say it, but there was an adversarial relationship between Richard and the club. And to a certain degree, there was a certain adversarial relationship between me and the club. But, hey, that's life. Everybody can't have suckers and pop all day. You've got to make the best of whatever your situation is. Ditka would kind of coddle McMichael and Fridge and give Richard and me the needle all of the time. And, you know, it worked. The bad blood, it was inevitable. You can't blame Richard for it. From Jerry Vainisi to Michael McCaskey to Ditka, I don't think they handled it the right way. But in the final analysis, Richard didn't go off the deep end, he didn't go crazy. He had a hell of a career.

As far as Richard's initial feeling of inferiority as an 8th-round draft pick from a small college coming into the NFL, I have come to this realization nearly 30 years later. If you work your ass off for four years in college, and you work yourself into position to become a first-rounder, God bless you. Nobody gives it to you. You did it yourself. Now, if you're an 8th-round pick, you have to work your ass off for four years in the NFL to make the same kind of money. It's either pay you now, after you finish your career in college as a first-round pick, or pay you later, after you earn it in the NFL. And now with the new rookie salary scale, it's going to be even more of the same. That's the way it is, and that's the way it's set up.

I know Richard resented it. Steve McMichael resented the fact that even though he was a second-round pick, he became a free agent after New England cut him. You lose a lot of your earning ability and command of the opportunity after you are cut by a team. You have to start over.

William Perry came in as a first-round draft pick and everything kind of fell into Fridge's lap. If you want to find something to get upset about, you can find it. You can worry about how people treat you, or what kind of shoulder pads they give you. I don't know if that was a huge impetus behind how Richard handled himself, but there is no question that if you are an 8th-round pick, you are not going to make the money. You're just worried about making the team. Once you make the team, then you have to become a starter, which he was that year. Then the next thing is, you have to be exceptional, which he was. So, what I did in college, becoming a nobody into a first-round pick, Richard basically had to do all over again with the Bears.

To have another teammate from the '85 Bears join me in the Pro Football Hall of Fame is phenomenal. You know, Mike Singletary was a great player. Was Mike Singletary a dynamo that you could have put on any defense and he would have made the Hall of Fame? Maybe not. Our defense afforded our linebackers a lot of opportunities. I will just say that. And that was our job. Mike Singletary is in the Hall of Fame, and that's super. But I am telling you that Richard Dent could have played for the Kansas City Chiefs, and he would have been in the Hall of Fame. He could have played for the Seattle Seahawks, and I think he would have been in the Hall of Fame. That's the difference in the kind of player Richard was.

He was exceptional. You got the pass-rusher you wanted, and the defense didn't have a liability as far as stopping the run. And here's the other thing: no man is an island. If you are a great pass-rusher, you are going to be double-teamed. That's what I loved about Steve McMichael, and that's what I loved about Richard. We had several players who commanded a double-team block, and that always left somebody one-on-one and ready to do damage. And that's why Richard Dent holds the Bears' all-time record for quarterback sacks.

AL HARRIS

When I arrived in Chicago in 1983 as an 8th-round draft pick, Al Harris had been switched from end to linebacker. Harris had been a first-round pick of the Bears and the 9th overall selection out of Arizona State in 1979.

Harris recorded nine sacks in 1982 and 1983, even though he had started in only about half of the games those two seasons. Al wound up playing 11 seasons in the NFL – nine with the Bears and his final two with the Philadelphia Eagles. At 6-5, 250 pounds, Harris was quick and agile enough to chase down a quarterback, bat down a pass attempt or pounce on a fumble. In fact, he had 10 career fumble recoveries and four interceptions.

Unfortunately, he missed the entire 1985 season, along with safety Todd Bell, because of a contract dispute. The strategy to hold out that year backfired on him and Todd. But Harris returned in 1986 and remained a key component until signing as a free agent with the Eagles prior to the '89 season. Al Harris served as an assistant coach to Mike Singletary with the San Francisco 49ers in recent years; he was the pass-rush coaching specialist for the 49ers. He also has done a great deal of motivational speaking and ministry.

As the son of a career Air Force man, Harris has lived in nine different states, including Hawaii, where he was born.

Harris, who lives with his wife Maggie, daughter Emily and son Jason, has spoken at churches, banquets, companies, corporations and charities, as well as speaking in chapels for professional baseball and football teams.

Now it is time for Al Harris to have his say about our time together with the Chicago Bears.

IN AL HARRIS's WORDS

I just remember that Richard Dent was a real green kid out of Tennessee State. He was real green and raw. And he was skinny back in those days. I remember thinking: *Wow, this kid is really undersized for a defensive end. But, boy, does he have a lot of talent.* I mean you could tell. The talent was oozing out of him.

But he was really raw as far as learning how to play the run. As far as rushing the passer, you saw some specialness to him right away. He had an incredible first step. His first step was probably as explosive as anyone's who played the game. You could see that right away in him.

What's funny about Richard is that we used to tease him. We used to call him Bad Body. He probably won't like me saying that. But we didn't say it in a bad way. It was just guys joking. When you looked at his body, he didn't have the traditional cut with the six-pack abdomen. You looked at some of those other young guys on the team who had worked out religiously and lifted weights, and they looked like they were chiseled out of granite or something. Richard didn't look like that. But, boy, did he play like that. And he was deceptively strong. When you looked at him, he didn't have defined structure to his musculature. But he was very, very strong for his size.

I did not sense back in the early '80s that Richard had any resentment toward his teammates who had been first-round draft picks, such as Dan Hampton and me. I mean, Richard and I got along very well. He came in as a defensive end in 1983. And that same year, I got moved to linebacker because we had a lot of injuries. So by the time Richard got into the swing of things, I was playing linebacker. I did not sense at that time that he was this bitter, frustrated athlete, or anything like that.

I was aware of the tension between him and Mike Ditka. When Ditka referred to Richard as Robert Dent, I didn't like it. You don't call somebody by a different name. I think Mike was trying to motivate Richard. And if you watch Richard walk, I kind of have a walk like that. It's a real relaxed walk and could be misperceived as being lazy. I can't speak for Mike Ditka, but I don't know if that played into it a little bit. But still, I think it was how Ditka said it. Sometimes you might joke about it and call somebody a different name as a friend, just from a teasing standpoint.

From Ditka's standpoint, I think he was trying to motivate Richard. But I would not have wanted someone to do that to me. That wouldn't be motivating for me. I wouldn't take it that way. I know that bothered Richard because I remember him talking to us about it at the time. It bothered me at the time, as well. I didn't like it. I don't know too many people who would like that. It wasn't just the fact that Ditka said the name "Robert Dent." It was how he said it. I would have chosen a different motivating tactic, personally, but I am not him. So I can't speak for Mike Ditka.

I will say that when the Bears defense really started to dominate in 1984, Richard was a gigantic piece of that. In 1983, we had a good defense. But the reason Richard did not start immediately in '83 was the fact that he did not know how to play against the long trap play. Or at least play it the way Buddy Ryan wanted him to play it. So Buddy would not put him in until Richard learned how to play the long trap in the running game. Now, once Richard learned how to play the long trap, Buddy put him in. If I remember right, Richard had 17 1/2 sacks in '84, and he got those sacks in just half a season. I mean, that has to be a record. I remember that last half of the season, he was absolutely insane as a pass-rusher. He was getting three to five sacks a game. He was doing it against teams like the Raiders and Minnesota. He was just dominating people.

I was playing linebacker at the time, and I knew in my mind when I was covering a receiver or a running back, I knew that ball had to be out of the quarterback's hand quickly because with guys around like Richard Dent, it was going to be a sack. Richard really, to me, turned our defense into a great defense, because you need that dominant pass-rusher. We did not have a dominant pass-rusher before that. We had some good pass-rushers, but we did not have a guy that you thought: *Oh, my gosh!* I mean, as great as Dan Hampton was, I don't think Hamp was a dominant pass-rusher. I think he was a very good pass-rusher, a very balanced player and a run-stopper. He gathered a lot of attention inside. But when you are talking about a pure, unadulterated pass-rusher, if you said, "Give me a pass-rusher," and it is third down, who would you pick out of all of the guys you have seen? I am picking Richard Dent. If you're talking pure, "Let's get a sack," that's who I am picking.

The key is that not only did he have the unbelievable first step, he also had incredible instincts and hands. His hands were so fast. And he really knew how to get separation between him and the blocker. And he was a very, very intelligent pass-rusher. A lot of times when people see a pass-rusher, they are thinking: *Ah, he's just doing it on instinct.* No, Richard understood blocking schemes. He understood what backs were trying to come at him and what angle they were going to try to take. He understood all of that stuff, and he put it all into a dynamite package. To me, he made that defense a great defense because of the presence he brought as far as putting pressure on the quarterback.

In addition to sacking quarterbacks and tipping passes, Richard had a great knack for stripping the ball out of the hands of quarterbacks and ballcarriers. Everybody talks about how Lawrence Taylor did that for the Giants. Richard was doing the very same thing right around the same time. And, you know, those are turnovers. Those are huge. It's not just getting a sack. When you turn the ball over, that's better than a sack. You could tell that Richard had played basketball in high school because his hands were soft for a big lineman. His quick-twitch muscles were outstanding, which were deceptive. Because when you looked at him, he had this big old bubble butt, skinny legs and his body was undefined. That's why we called him Bad Body. It didn't look like the traditional athletic body. But, boy, could he play.

Richard's production defied his slow, easy-going walk, because once he turns it on, he gets to a whole other level. The other point to be made is that Richard's aggressiveness and ability to create turnovers affected the production of his teammates, as well. When you have a force like that on your team, other players on the opposition have to account for him. Richard's presence and ability allowed me to know that if I was in coverage or rushing the passer and I am grabbing a guy, you know there is going to be a high probability of at least getting pressure, if not a sack or a turnover.

As our defensive unit was being formed, Buddy Ryan was looking at the whole system. He wasn't looking at just one person. That's why he waited for Richard to improve his reaction to the trap play before he allowed him to start. Actually, Richard and I had the same problem learning how to defend the long trap because we played it with the wrong shoulder; we played it with the inside shoulder. In college, I was taught to use the inside shoulder, just like Richard. So I struggled with it initially, too.

When the long trap would come my way, I just slid down and threw my inside flipper, and we were taught to nail the inside guy in there. But what Buddy wanted us to do, he wanted us to see the guy bounced and let the linebackers run the guy down. The way defensive ends were taught to play the trap back in those days was to use the inside shoulder. So it was awkward at first with the Bears.

Richard and I were so fast and agile, we felt like, we could run them down ourselves. Why should we bounce it to the linebacker? I can't speak for Richard, but I know that is what I was thinking. And I wouldn't doubt that it was what Richard was thinking. It might have taken Richard a little longer to figure out how to defend the long trap because he might have been stubborn. Maybe he just wanted to do it his way. But Buddy would always say, "You're not getting in, son, until you learn how to play the long trap." I think most people would tell you that was the issue.

I am absolutely surprised it took Richard so long to get inducted into the Pro Football Hall of Fame. I am not disrespecting some of the guys who got inducted before Richard, but when you look at a guy who had 137 sacks, a Super Bowl MVP award on a Super Bowl winner and was a key member of one of the most dominating defenses of all-time, if he is not a first-ballot Hall of Famer, he is definitely a second ballot Hall of Famer. So I was kind of concerned that he was going to be bypassed. It didn't make any sense to me. There is no question in my mind that he is a Hall of Famer.

OTIS WILSON

One of the pillars of our Chicago Bears defense was outside linebacker Otis Wilson, who remains a good friend of mine to this day.

Otis was a first-round draft pick out of Louisville in 1980, and he quickly established himself as a quick, strong and savvy defender. He teamed up with Mike Singletary and Wilber Marshall as a stout linebacking corps. He had 10.5 sacks in a memorable 1985 season.

During his nine-season career, Otis wound up with 36 sacks, 8 fumble recoveries, 10 interceptions and 2 touchdowns in 110 games.

IN OTIS WILSON'S WORDS

Richard was a guy who came into the league as an 8th-round pick and weighed about 220 or 230, if that much. If you just looked at him then, you would say that this guy wasn't going to pan out to be anything. But his hard work and dedication, and his willingness to go to the training table to put some weight on him … I mean, it turned out to be a blessing. Richard was the consummate professional. He is a great person in his own right, but also a hell of an athlete. He made you step your game up.

He always has been articulate and knowledgeable about the game, and he played it at one level. I think he should have gotten more publicity than he has gotten, but our head coach really suppressed a lot of us. He really didn't want us to get our just due. When you look at the Lawrence Taylors and the Reggie Whites … you know, Richard is up there with those guys. When you talk about those guys, you should be talking about Richard Dent. A lot of guys on our defense were headstrong black men, and a lot of people don't like that, especially the Chicago Bears organization and Mike Ditka. It was about them, instead of about what we were doing to make them a better organization. Because I always say that it goes both ways.

Richard, whenever he stepped onto that field, whenever he was in practice, was always a professional. He always listened. He always made suggestions. We made each other better. There were certain situations where I would line up on his side sometimes, because obviously Wilber Marshall was on that side the most. But I would look down that line and tell Richard, "I'm coming to get the quarterback, and I am going to be there before you."

He would look at me and laugh. He would say, "Yeah, right. This sack is mine." We challenged each other like that because I wasn't going to let him get all of the publicity. I've got to get some, too. So we pushed one another, and he played the game at one speed. Sometimes he would have problems with the coach, and when people have that question mark about you, they will suppress you. They will say certain things, do certain things.

Of all of the people on our defense, the only one who got all the publicity he was supposed to was Mike Singletary.

To me, Richard deserves to be a Hall of Famer. He played like that, he worked like that. I've got nothing bad to say about my man. That's my road dog.

When people criticized Richard for taking plays off, they need to understand that the player on the other side of the ball is getting paid, too. He is the best at what he does. So as a defensive end, if you come in rushing him the same way every time, the other player is no dummy, and he is going to figure that out.

Richard always told me that you have to have three or four different moves, and that you have to figure out when to use those moves, how to use those moves, and it depends on who you are facing. Everybody has a different offensive style. Every opponent has different strengths and weaknesses. Anybody who would ever say that Richard would take plays off is wrong. That is what we called lulling the opponent to sleep. I have never seen Richard take a play off. As a matter of fact, you had to back him down sometimes.

There were so many times that Richard was listed as a finalist to make the Hall of Fame but did not make the final cut. That was tough because many times we were ready to celebrate. But it was up to the selection committee and the process to make that determination. There were so many times when you saw some other players get into the Hall of Fame, and you would look at the credentials Richard had and we were all frustrated sometimes.

I kept telling Richard that he would go into the Hall of Fame eventually. We had one of the great defenses in NFL history, and one thing I can say for certain is that no defense dominated the way we did. Many teams won football games; we dominated football games. Sometimes it was almost reminiscent of former heavyweight boxing champ Mike Tyson during his heyday. When people stepped in the ring against Tyson, you knew the fight was over, because that guy just did away with them. And that's what we did.

For that one year in 1985 of the Super Bowl, and the three years leading up to it, I don't think anybody … and I am going back into the '60s and leading up to 1985 … was as dominant as we were. That is something no one can ever take away.

Do you have some other multiple championship teams that played some damn good football? They played good football, but they didn't knock the snot out of people like we did. I'll take my hat off to that because no one can deny that.

There has been a lot of talk about the New Orleans Saints' bounty system and the fact that their former defensive coordinator, Gregg Williams, used strong language to motivate his players, even to the point of offering money and telling his players to intentionally injure the opponent.

I have heard worse language than that. But you don't take it literally to the point of trying to hurt somebody. I certainly remember our game against the Green Bay Packers when Charles Martin threw Jim McMahon to the ground well after he released the ball. Martin had a hit list with the numbers written on a towel around his waist of the Bears he wanted to take out and hurt.

This is a violent game. People come to the stadium to see that long ball thrown, that big hit when the fans can go, "Ooooh!" and to see the running back score that 30-yard touchdown. The coaches have always said to us, "I want that guy on the ground. I don't care how you get him on the ground." Or that quarterback. Or that wide receiver. They would tell us to kick the you-know-what out of him. Coaches say things because they are emotional.

I don't think you go out there with the intent of trying to hurt somebody. As far as what the defensive coordinator said in New Orleans, that's nothing that somebody else hadn't said in the past. All teams do that, whether it is the head coach or the players. I think those fines were excessive, but this is the nature of the beast. But if you are literally going out there to injure somebody, then that's a different story.

I was watching the New Orleans Saints, even when they won the Super Bowl. They weren't really knocking the hell out of anybody. I mean, they were getting people on the ground, but I didn't see any vicious hits. I just think that sometimes what is said in the locker room stays in the locker room. I didn't see a whole lot of illegal or vicious hits.

When Richard and I played with the Bears, the game was always a smash-mouth contest, and yet we played it the right way. Whatever was said in the locker room was only intended to get people fired up, and obviously it worked for us big time.

———◉———

Many exceptional football players come from smaller colleges and simply need an opportunity to prove themselves on the NFL level. Here I am, #95, set to deliver a blow in a college game against Tennessee-Chattanooga.

There are some proud snapshot moments in life that you wish you could freeze and hold onto forever. Being serenaded by fans and well-wishers during the Hall of Fame parade was one of those very special occasions. And being able to share that entire weekend experience with my former coach at Tennessee State, Joe Gilliam, made it even more memorable. I was thrilled that members of the Tennessee State marching band and bus-loads of others from my alma mater took part in the Hall of Fame parade and weekend festivities.

While I enjoyed great success in the NFL, nothing can replicate the feeling of camaraderie I enjoyed during my years at Tennessee State. I wore number 95 in college and continued to wear that number in the NFL.

Clyde Emrich, who was one of the NFL's first strength coaches, worked with many Bears players during his more than 40 years with the organization. He was an Olympic weight lifter himself. Emrich told the media that I was one of the strongest Bears players he ever worked with during his career.

(Standing) Local news reporter. (L. to R.) Michael Jordan's mother, my mom, and the mothers of Andre Dawson and Dennis McKinnon were treated royally for a TV show called "Superstars and their Moms" in 1989. It was my mother's first trip to Chicago, and she would pass away three weeks later.

(Left) Tyrone Keys was a respected teammate of mine on the Chicago Bears from 1983-85 when I was just becoming accustomed to the NFL. He also appeared in the Super Bowl Shuffle video that we taped toward the end of the '85 season. Tyrone later played on the defensive line for Tampa Bay and San Diego.

(Right) Michael McCaskey was president of the Bears during my playing career in Chicago, and he was the man in charge when we captured Super Bowl XX. He is the oldest grandchild of George Halas and a son of Virginia Halas McCaskey. I thanked the McCaskey family during my Hall of Fame acceptance speech, including another son Brian McCaskey, who was in attendance in Canton, Ohio. The McCaskeys took a chance on a skinny kid who showed potential coming out of a small college in Tennessee, and I hope I was able to repay their faith and trust in me.

There are so many memories for me growing up in the South. In 1968, my brothers and I planted this pecan tree that grew this tall by 2008. I now own this property in Avondale, Ga., where the famous movie "Driving Miss Daisy" was filmed.

I am proud of this 1950 Mercury that I rebuilt for my collection in 1987. That was also the year that I rebuilt my reputation around the NFL as a reliable player and solid citizen.

Back in 1986 when this picture was taken, I got a jump-start on my friend Michael Jordan in terms of world championships after the Bears won Super Bowl XX. Of course, Jordan went on to lead the Chicago Bulls to six NBA titles beginning in 1991. Michael is one of the most generous and loyal people I have had the pleasure to know. Physically, he is the most freakishly gifted. Here we are at an event with our friend, former Packers safety, Daryll Jones. Hard to believe 26 years have passed by so quickly.

Here's the scene at Fawcett Stadium in Canton, Ohio, hours before the induction ceremony in August, 2011. The seats are beginning to fill up and I am eagerly anticipating giving my acceptance speech in front of friends, family and millions of television viewers.

Shortly after I received the official word that I had been elected to the Hall of Fame, the Chicago Bears hosted a press conference for me at Halas Hall in Lake Forest, Illinois. It was another proud moment for me, and I could not conceal my elation

It was nice to see that Mike Ditka and Buddy Ryan (front and center) had set aside their differences when we all gathered

Jim McMahon was our starting quarterback on the Super Bowl XX champs, and he made a lot of clutch plays during his injury-plagued career. I felt that I was just as much of a difference-maker for the Bears on defense and should have been paid accordingly. During our 25-year reunion, McMahon told the *Chicago Tribune* that he was having short-term memory issues.

Mike Ditka was all smiles at our 25-year Super Bowl reunion in Chicago. There was a reason we all nicknamed him Sybil, because of the multiple personalities he would display on a regular basis.

25-year reunion of the Super Bowl XX champs.

(Right) I maintain a great interest in the Better Boys Foundation, as well as my Make a Dent Foundation. Helping young people learn how to improve their circumstances in life is crucial to the future of our country. In this photo I am shown with my friend Jack Kellman from the BBF during our trip to Cuba as we explored opportunities there.

In 1987, we were still the toast of the town in Chicago since we had just won a Super Bowl the year before. Former Bears cornerback Michael Richardson (L) is shown here with Scott Julian, Willie Gault and me at the Grammy Awards ceremony. We always displayed a swagger on and off the field.

Something seems to have caught the eye of President Clinton in this 1993 photo as I accompany him. When it comes to sports and politics, people are really passionate in Chicago. President Clinton is a great sports fan, as well.

My former teammate Dave Duerson (L) and former Chicago School Board president Rufus Williams helped me celebrate at my 40th birthday party in Chicago. Duerson always appeared to be such a confident and secure person, both on and off the field. I guess I never will understand why he took his own life.

I will be forever grateful to the McCaskey family for their support throughout the years. Pat McCaskey (L) is the grandson of Bears founder and NFL pioneer George Halas. And Virginia McCaskey was the daughter of Halas and the matriarch of the Bears organization. I appreciate the fact that the McCaskeys kept the legacy of George Halas alive to help young men reach their potential.

I was humbled to be a part of the 2011 Pro Football Hall of Fame induction class that included: (L. to R.) Chris Hanburger, Les Richter (represented by his son Jon Richter), Shannon Sharpe, me, Marshall Faulk and Deion Sanders. Not shown was inductee Ed Sabol, the man behind the idea of NFL Films that won 52 Emmy awards. It was quite an impressive stage to share.

(Left) Being elected to the Pro Football Hall of Fame introduced me to a special fraternity of athletes who take their inclusion quite seriously. Here I am shaking hands with former New York Giants halfback Frank Gifford, who went on to fame as a Monday Night Football analyst. Gifford was inducted into the Hall of Fame in 1977.

(Right) Success on the football field doesn't always translate to success in the business world. But I have been fortunate to meet influential people from all walks of life as a result of my status as a former NFL player. The older I get, the more I cherish those relationships and appreciate what everyone brings to the table to improve our communities.

Joe Gilliam Sr. had so much to do with my development as a football player and a man at Tennessee State. To have him present me at the Pro Football Hall of Fame made me feel incredible. He was a defensive coordinator and later the head coach at Tennessee State from 1989-1992. He is the father of the late Pittsburgh Steelers quarterback Joe Gilliam.

There was nothing more gratifying for me than to see that look of desperation on the face of an opposing quarterback once I had him in my sights. I have former Washington Redskins quarterback Joe Theismann on the run here, and I am determined to lower the boom.

I have been in the energy management business for the past ten years as the CEO of RLD Resources, LLC.. Dependability and respect mean a lot to me as a businessman, just as that reputation meant so much to me as a football player.

I am blessed to have two young sons: Shiloh, left (with my girlfriend DeEtta Jones) and R.J., right. I want them to have every opportunity to succeed in life.

Many friends helped me celebrate my Hall of Fame induction in Canton, Ohio, including (from my left) Jim Reynolds – the founder and CEO of Loop Capital Markets, LLC and former Bears teammates Tyrone Keys, Mike Richardson, Otis Wilson and Jim Covert.

So many impactful people in my football life and personal life were on hand to wish me well at the Hall of Fame in 2011. Here's (L. to R.) my former coach Joe Gilliam, girlfriend DeEtta Jones, daughter Sarah, my father Horace, me and my daughter Mary.

Super Memories 9

I was fortunate to play 15 seasons in the NFL with the Chicago Bears, San Francisco 49ers, Philadelphia Eagles, and Indianapolis Colts. In my career, I earned two Super Bowl rings, one with the Bears following the 1985 season and another with the 49ers in 1994, even though I was injured much of that season.

But to this day, the questions I am asked the most have to do with the Super Bowl XX champion Bears. There was something about that team. It had lasting qualities that seemed to appeal to people around the world. And just think, we won during an era that actually preceded the Internet Age! In fact, there were no cell phone cameras then. No Facebook or Twitter, no real social media. Considering some of the mischief and wild things that went on with that Bears team, perhaps it is just as well.

Our team was full of characters and eccentric personalities. Mike Ditka, our head coach, seemed to lead the way. He had boisterous daily exchanges with the local and national media. One day he was roller-skating in the office building at Halas Hall in Lake Forest, Illinois;

another day he was taking the chewing gum out of his mouth and throwing it at a visiting fan who was heckling him after a Bears loss. Ditka often would chastise a sportswriter, and he came close to exchanging punches with our defensive coordinator, Buddy Ryan, during halftime of our loss to Miami in 1985. There certainly wasn't a dull moment when it came to Ditka or our team.

Ditka once said, "In life, there are teams called Smith and teams called 'Grabowski. We're Grabowskis!"

We became the toast of the town in 1985, often making luncheon and banquet appearances. Some guys on the team had regular radio or television gigs. We had a lot of rollicking bravado and we weren't afraid to show it, on or off the field.

A lot of fans and media refer to that Bears team as one of the most dominant in NFL history. After all, we averaged 28.5 points a game on offense (second in the NFL). On defense, we limited our opponents to just 12.4 points a game, which was tops in the NFL that season. We had a takeaway/giveaway ratio of plus-23, which was first in the NFL. We finished the regular season with a 15-1 record, and then breezed through the postseason by out-scoring our opponents 91-10. I would have to say that was about as dominant a performance as you can have in an NFL season.

Our defense forced 54 turnovers. During one stretch, we went two months without giving up more than 10 points in a game.

If William "The Refrigerator" Perry wasn't stuffing a running back or harassing the quarterback, he was catching a touchdown pass or diving into the end zone for a score as a fullback on offense. It was that kind of bizarre year when everything we tried seemed to work perfectly.

I am particularly proud of my performance in the playoffs that year. Against the New York Giants in the divisional playoff game at Soldier Field, I was credited with seven tackles, 3.5 sacks, and two forced fumbles.

Following the 21-0 shutout of the Giants was the NFC Championship Game against the Los Angeles Rams. Wilber Marshall and I were able to team up for what many consider the pivotal play of that postseason. Late in the fourth quarter it began to snow. Rams quarterback Dieter Brock dropped back to pass, and I rushed and sacked him, knocking the ball loose. Marshall picked up the loose ball and returned it for a touchdown as I escorted him down the field with Otis Wilson and other blockers.

One of the signature defensive plays of our Bears championship season occurred in the NFC Championship game against the Rams at Soldier Field. I sacked quarterback Dieter Brock, causing a fumble that was recovered by linebacker Wilber Marshall. He returned the fumble 52 yards for a touchdown in the fourth quarter and we all rejoiced.
(Photo courtesy of Mike Kinyon)

Sportswriters later wrote that the late George Halas was signaling his approval at that moment with the snow flakes. We blanked the Rams, 24-0.

During Super Bowl XX, I shared two sacks, forced two fumbles, and blocked a pass.

Along with the team's success in 1985 came a ton of individual accolades:

- Mike Singletary was named NFC Defensive Player of the Year.
- Walter Payton was honored as NFC Offensive Player of the Year.
- Ditka was NFL Coach of the Year.
- I was named the Super Bowl MVP.

Most Bears fans remember the final score of Super Bowl XX because we shellacked the New England Patriots, 46-10. But here are the official details according to the Associated Press.

Super Bowl XX: Chicago Bears 46, New England Patriots 10

	1	2	3	4	Total
Bears	13	10	21	2	46
Patriots	3	0	0	7	10

at Louisiana Superdome, New Orleans, Louisiana

Game time: 5:25 p.m. EST/4:25 p.m. CST

Referee: Red Cashion

TV announcers (NBC): Dick Enberg, Merlin Olsen, and Bob Griese

Scoring

- NE – Tony Franklin 36 yd FG (NE 3-0)
- CHI – Kevin Butler 28 yd FG (3-3)
- CHI – Kevin Butler 24 yd FG (CHI 6-3)
- CHI – Matt Suhey 11 yd TD run (Butler kick) (CHI 13-3)
- CHI – Jim McMahon 2 yd TD run (Butler kick) (CHI 20-3)
- CHI – Kevin Butler 24 yd FG (CHI 23-3)
- CHI – Jim McMahon 1 yd TD run (Butler kick) (CHI 30-3)
- CHI – Reggie Phillips 28 yd interception return TD (Butler kick) (CHI 37-3)
- CHI – William Perry 1 yd TD run (Butler kick) (CHI 44-3)
- NE – 8 yd TD pass from Steve Grogan to Irving Fryar (Franklin kick) (CHI 44-10)
- CHI – Safety, Steve Grogan sacked in end zone by Henry Waechter (CHI 46-10)

The fact that we were unable to win multiple Super Bowls, largely because McMahon was frequently injured, showed what an impact he had on our offense. He was known as the Punky QB, and he had his own way of doing things. I saw him take some tough hits and have to endure a lot from a physical standpoint.

One of the remarkable aspects of our Bears teams was that everyone played an important role in the team's success, including backup running back and kick returner Dennis Gentry. His nickname was "Pinky" and we always could count on him to come up with a clutch third-down play or something to spark the offense and special teams. He even appeared in our Super Bowl Shuffle video, pretending to play the bass.

In 1985, McMahon played in 13 of our 16 regular-season games. He started 11 of them. He threw for 15 touchdowns and had 11 intercepted while winding up with a passer rating of 82.6.

Perhaps the most memorable game for Jim was against the Vikings in the third game of the season. I remember that it was a Thursday night game in Minneapolis and that Steve Fuller started because McMahon was injured. We were trailing, 17-9, in the third quarter and it looked as if we were going to lose for the first time that season.

McMahon somehow convinced Ditka that he was able to play, and he proceeded to throw three touchdown passes in the third quarter. His first pass was to Willie Gault for 70 yards. Then came a 25-yarder to Dennis McKinnon, followed by a 43-yard TD pass to McKinnon. The game ended with us beating the Vikings 33-24, giving us a 3-0 record.

Whenever a team can pull out an improbable victory like that, everyone gains tremendous confidence.

I remember how pumped we were to win that game – both the offense and the defense. Scoring 24 points in the third quarter alone seemed impossible before McMahon entered the game. He seemed to provide so much energy to that side of the ball, and there was no doubt that he was considered a leader.

Being the backup for McMahon was no easy task. Steve Fuller had to be ready at a moment's notice to step in if McMahon got hurt, and that happened a few times during the 1985 season.

Fuller played seven seasons in the NFL, and he was our backup quarterback from 1984-86. He played his college ball at Clemson University. Before coming to the Bears, Fuller had played for the Kansas City Chiefs and Los Angeles Rams.

While he was not at McMahon's level as a player, Fuller did fill in well at times, including starting in our 44-0 victory over the Dallas Cowboys in 1985. The Cowboys were known as "America's Team" at the time, and it was particularly gratifying to knock them off their perch.

What an important victory that was for our franchise! The Cowboys had beaten the Bears in six straight previous matchups.

Gary Fencik, our Pro Bowl safety at the time, was asked recently about that game and said, "I remember saying if we win this week, I think we have a chance to go to the Super Bowl. Little did I know that it would be that convincing."

"That was the first time I had beaten the Cowboys in the preseason, regular season, or post-season in my career, and I was in my 10th year. It was a pretty memorable game. Buddy Ryan took me out and I wouldn't go out because I had not beaten the Cowboys," says Fencik.

Fuller completed just 9 of 24 passes in that one-sided victory for us, but no one in Chicago cared about his individual stats after that win in Dallas. Walter Payton led the Bears offense, rushing for 132 yards to become the first player in NFL history to top 1,000 yards in nine seasons.

Our defense was as dominant that day as I had ever seen it.

We recorded six sacks, four interceptions, and one fumble recovery and scored the game's first two touchdowns on interception returns, one by me and the other by Mike Richardson. Otis Wilson twice knocked Dallas quarterback Danny White out of the game.

After the game, Ditka told the media, "I thought the defense was going to outscore the offense for a while there." The victory also meant something special to Ditka personally because his former coach and mentor was Tom

Landry of the Cowboys. Ditka also had served as special teams coach under Landry in Dallas.

Fuller didn't wind up with the greatest career stats, but on that one day in Dallas, he definitely got the job done.

I can also relate to the difficult path Mike Tomzcak had to take to carve out a long career in the NFL. While I was an 8th-round draft pick from Tennessee State, Tomczak was a free agent quarterback out of Ohio State.

As a rookie, Tomczak did not start any games for us in 1985, but he did make some appearances, including one in the fourth quarter of Super Bowl XX. He played for us from 1985-90 before making other NFL stops in Green Bay, Cleveland, Pittsburgh, and Detroit.

Tomczak received more playing time in Pittsburgh, starting most of the season and helping the Steelers make the playoffs.

Not bad for a guy who wasn't even drafted.

I even remember Tomczak being part of the Shufflin Crew© video – he mimicked playing the guitar.

Mike wound up starting 31 games for the Bears, throwing 31 touchdowns. Problem was, he also threw 47 interceptions.

With the Bears, I remember that Tomczak won his first 10 starts, which set an NFL record that has since been broken by Ben Roethlisberger of the Steelers.

One of Tomczak's most famous starts came in the 1988 playoff game against the Philadelphia Eagles. That game has been dubbed the Fog Bowl.

I can see that game in my mind's eye better than I could actually see the field that strange day. It was New Year's Eve, and we wound up winning 20-12. Fog set in over Soldier Field during the second half.

In the third quarter, Tomczak was knocked out of action with a bruised left shoulder when the Eagles' 285-pound All-Pro Reggie White landed on him just after he threw a pass that was intercepted. McMahon, appearing for the first time since his knee was severely sprained October 30, took over for

Tomczak, completed two of three passes and directed a run-dominated 70-yard drive to a closing field goal by Kevin Butler.

The Eagles' quarterback, Randall Cunningham, completed 27 of 54 passes for 407 yards, but the NFC East champion Eagles repeatedly self-destructed when they had opportunities to score.

Dropped passes, bungled assignments, and costly penalties underscored the Eagles' playoff inexperience. Twelve times they moved into Bear territory, eight times inside the 30, and all they could get was four field goals.

Twice, on consecutive plays, the Eagles had touchdown passes wiped out by penalties on fullback Anthony Toney. Then they lost one when tight end Keith Jackson dropped the ball in the end zone. They also missed by about a half-inch on Cunningham's fourth-down sneak at our 4-yard line, and killed another TD threat with offensive pass interference.

By 1988, Buddy Ryan was the head coach of the Eagles, which made this game even more emotional for me.

"You can't blame this loss on the weather, but I could hardly see across the field, and I'm sure they couldn't, either," Ryan said after the loss. "They'd run a play, and I didn't know who had the ball or what the hell was going on."

League officials were at the game and contemplated suspending it. But referee Jim Tunney advised them that conditions at field level were acceptable.

"There was no reason for the game to be suspended," said Ryan. "If this was a baseball game, maybe. But this is football, and you have to play the game."

Tomczak was injured after completing 10 of 20 passes for 172 yards, 64 coming on an early TD pass to Dennis McKinnon. He had three passes intercepted, matching Cunningham's total.

"A win's a win, baby," Tomczak said after that game.

Tomczak joked about the role reversal of McMahon replacing him.

"Let No. 9 go in and try winning one for me," said Tomczak. "I've been saving his rear end for the last four years."

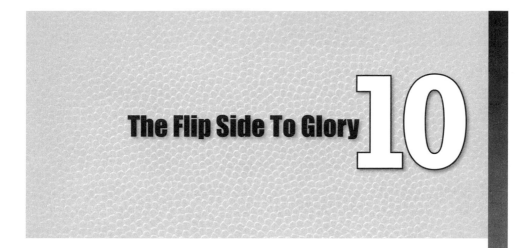

The Flip Side To Glory 10

At the end of the day, each team in the NFL should put up $2 million over five years to go toward the players who are going through medical issues, since we don't have health insurance after playing. Give that money to the insurance company and let the games go on. If it were the food industry they would shut it down. If it were the car industry, they would stop making cars. But guys in the NFL are dying and they don't give a damn. The NFL doesn't care, they just want to protect their pocket book.

Jim McMahon disclosed to the *Chicago Tribune* during our 25-year Super Bowl anniversary celebration that he was having problems remembering things after all of the concussions he had suffered as a player.

"Back then, it was just tape an aspirin to your helmet and you go back in," McMahon said. "I've worked with some neurosurgeons and it's a very serious thing, man.

"My memory's pretty much gone. There are a lot of times when I walk into a room and forget why I walked in there. I'm going through some studies right now and I am going to do a brain scan. It's unfortunate what the game does to you."

McMahon joined the Bears in 1982, but it wasn't until 1988 that he was able to start the first seven games of a season.

That 1988 season was especially treacherous for NFL quarterbacks.

Including McMahon, seven quarterbacks were knocked out of games in the sixth week of that season. Detroit's Chuck Long (knee), Cleveland's Mike Pagel (shoulder), San Francisco's Joe Montana (ribs), Houston's Cody Carlson (thumb), Indianapolis' Chris Chandler (sternum), and San Diego's Babe Laufenberg (ribs) went down for the count.

McMahon suffered a mild concussion in the second quarter of our 24-7 victory over Detroit. McMahon probably could have returned in the second half if Mike Tomczak had not performed so well and kept us in command.

Still, it was important that McMahon start games for us. The Bears had a 32-3 regular-season record in the previous 35 games he had started.

Ditka said then that he was confident McMahon would be ready for the next game.

"McMahon is fine, he's going to play, he's going to practice," Ditka told the media.

"He had a concussion, but it cleared by halftime, said trainer Fred Caito. "He lost his memory a little bit."

Since being drafted in the first round out of Brigham Young in 1982, McMahon underwent the usual NFL quarterback torture test and emerged with knee, shoulder, and hand injuries. In addition, he suffered his lacerated kidney in 1984.

I can certainly relate to what Jim is going through as a former NFL player. I have agreed to go through similar brain trauma studies at Boston University.

Football is a violent game that all of us in the National Football League signed up to play with our eyes wide open. As grown men, we knew of the potential dangers and hazards and the very real possibility of serious and perhaps even permanent damage that could be done to our bodies.

Along with the advancements in the quality of equipment over the years, the players have gotten faster and stronger with each generation, but the human joints, particularly the knees and shoulders, can take only so much force and pressure. Something has to give, regardless of how much padding and artificial reinforcements are in place.

Helmets have much better padding and protective coverings now than even when I played in the '80s and '90s. Yet we still see serious head and spinal injuries practically every week of the NFL season.

In recent years, a number of rules changes have been legislated by the NFL with the purpose of reducing the risk factors for serious head injuries. Sadly, I have seen first-hand in recent months how the cumulative effect of blows to the head have, over a period of time, adversely affected the lives of former teammates and opposing players.

When I think about the vicious hits administered by some of the '85 Bears defenders, I have to wonder how many fines and suspensions would have been levied on them. Safety Gary Fencik was renowned for being a hard hitter. He and safety Doug Plank were known as "The Hitmen" in the early 80s. Plank, in particular, routinely led with his helmet after taking a running start to blast a receiver or ballcarrier. He retired in 1982, a year before I joined the Bears.

It was the aggressive nature of Plank, who wore jersey No. 46, that inspired Buddy Ryan to name our attack defense the 46 Defense.

Plank talked in great deal about the violent nature of the NFL game when he played for the Bears. He said in a *Chicago Tribune* article that he could not recall just how many concussions he had sustained during his career, noting that the football culture was different then. Players were said to be dinged up or they had their bell rung, when actually they may have sustained a concussion that should have warranted more serious medical attention.

Plank said he was fined by the NFL just once for a hit that did not even draw a penalty flag. He also regrets one of his most devastating hits.

"We're all players, and we're all trying to accomplish the same thing to help our team win and make the fans happy. At a certain point, there is an accountability factor, too."

I can certainly relate to Plank's sentiments. It is a dog-eat-dog game of survival out on the football field. Plank said that his survival instincts would kick in on the field and that it was not natural human behavior for football players to get a running start and run into someone with intent to do bodily harm.

Plank was generously listed in the game programs as being 6-feet, 200 pounds. Because he was actually smaller than most of the receivers and running backs he had to tackle, Plank felt he had to use his head and helmet as a weapon to make his presence felt.

"I knocked myself out many times in running into a player," he was quoted as saying. "Everyone thinks, just because you are on defense, the damage is one-sided, that it's all on the offensive players. I've got three joints replaced- two shoulders and a knee. I'm probably going to need three more in the next five years. So this isn't a one-sided issue."

Amen.

Mike Singletary also was known as a hard hitter, although he seldom led with the crown of his helmet.

In early 2011, the 32 NFL owners voted unanimously to approve rules amendments for player safety. One of the changes includes outlawing a player launching himself into a defenseless opponent. A 15-yard penalty will result for anyone who leaves both feet before contact to spring forward and upward into an opponent to deliver a blow to the helmet with any part of his helmet.

In addition, such tackles will be subject to fines. The NFL really got serious about flagrant hits in 2010, increasing the amount of fines and threatening suspensions. Ray Anderson is the NFL s chief disciplinarian. He said suspensions will be considered for "egregious hits" this season.

The definition of a defenseless receiver has been further defined. Now, a receiver who has not had time to protect himself or has not clearly become a runner, even if both feet are on the ground, is considered defenseless.

Defenseless players cannot be hit in the head or neck area with the helmet, facemask, forearm or shoulder. The definition of such players now includes those throwing a pass; attempting or completing a catch without having time to ward off or avoid contact; a runner whose forward progress has been stopped by a tackler; kickoff or punt returners while the ball is in the air; kickers or punters during a kick or a return; a quarterback during a change of possession; a player who receives a blindside block from a blocker moving toward his own end zone.

Also, hits to the head of a passer that are not considered "forcible" blows will not be penalized. Penalized players are subject to being ejected for flagrant penalties.

"Rule-wise, I think the competition committee is clear that we are not trying to change rules, but change the emphasis, and that message has been delivered loud and clear to the players," committee co-chairman Rich McKay, president of the Atlanta Falcons, told reporters. "I was encouraged as a committee member who watched all the video at the end of last year to look at injuries, and I thought the players did a good job of understanding the message and adapting to it."

Another significant rules change beginning with the 2011 season involved moving the spot of the kickoff from the 30 to the 35-yard line. Once again, the idea behind it is to limit the number of kick returns, where many injuries seem to occur. NFL kickers are more likely to be able to kick the ball into or through the end zone more often, forcing the receiving team to take the touchback and place the ball on their own 20-yard line.

This new rule met with great resistance from some teams such as the Bears, who have prospered in the past with an effective kickoff return unit headed by Devin Hester and Danieal Manning.

"I don't like the rule," Seahawks kick returner Leon Washington said on the ESPN Radio show in Seattle. "And I'm sure (the New York Jets') Brad Smith and (Chicago's) Devin Hester and (Cleveland's) Joshua Cribbs and the rest of those guys that do a really good job of returning the ball don't like the rule. It's part of the game that's really exciting. I think fans look forward to it because it's an instant momentum-changer."

Initially, the league's competition committee proposed moving touchbacks up to the 25, eliminating the blocking wedge and limiting coverage players from long run-ups. The league reduced the number of players allowed in a blocking wedge to two in 2009.

However, several coaches were concerned about making too many changes on kickoffs, thinking that bringing touchbacks out to the 25 would affect field position too much. Coaches are worried about an increase in touchbacks from 16 percent in 2010.

The owners voted 26-6 for the new rule.

"The bottom line is it's ... the highest risk of injury play," said New Orleans Saints coach Sean Payton.

Hester has an NFL-record 14 touchdowns on kick returns.

"They might as well put up the Arena (Football League) nets (behind the end zones), man, because there's going to be a lot of balls going in the end zone ...," Hester said on Chicago's ESPN Radio program. "They're going too far. They're changing the whole fun of the game. Fans come out to see, especially to Chicago, to see returns. That's one of the key aspects to our team. Fans love our big returns, and taking that out of the game makes for a lesser game."

In 2009, NFL teams were issued stricter instructions as far as when players should be allowed to return to games or practices after sustaining head injuries.

Commissioner Roger Goodell sent a memo to the 32 clubs saying a player who gets a concussion should not return to action on the same day if he shows certain signs or symptoms.

Those signs include an inability to remember assignments or plays, a gap in memory, persistent dizziness, and persistent headaches.

The old concussion response standard, established in 2007, stipulated that a player should not be allowed to return to the same game if he lost consciousness.

Goodell s memo also stated that players "are to be encouraged to be candid with team medical staffs and fully disclose any signs or symptoms that may be associated with a concussion."

According to an Associated Press survey in 2009, nearly one-fifth of 160 NFL players replied that they had hidden or played down the effects of a concussion.

The league said its concussion committee, team doctors, outside medical experts and the NFL Players Association worked on the new standards.

NFLPA assistant executive director George Atallah responded by saying the union is "encouraged by this new policy." Atallah added that the NFLPA "will continue to examine these issues independently to recommend the best possible policies and procedures."

The new policy states, in part: "Once removed for the duration of a practice or game, the player should not be considered for return-to-football activities until he is fully asymptomatic, both at rest and after exertion, has a normal neurological examination, normal neuropsychological testing, and has been cleared to return by both his team physician(s) and the independent neurological consultant."

NFL teams also were told they have to find an outside neurologist who can be consulted on concussions. NFL spokesman Greg Aiello said all of those independent doctors had been approved and were in place.

"The evidence demonstrates that team medical staffs have been addressing concussions in an increasingly cautious and conservative way," Goodell wrote in the memo to teams. "This new return-to-play statement reinforces our commitment to advancing player safety. Along with improved equipment, better education, and rules changes designed to reduce impacts to the head, it will make our game safer for the men who play it, and set an important example for players at all levels of play." If you want to make the game safer, the offensive player should not be allowed to lower his head on a defensive player, and vice-versa.

One of the early symbols of the viciousness of pro football was the late Darryl Stingley, who lost the use of his limbs playing the game at the age of 27.

A product of Chicago's West Side, Stingley was a promising NFL wide receiver with the New England Patriots. A Marshall High School and Purdue alum, Stingley was paralyzed from a vicious tackle by the Oakland Raiders' Jack Tatum during an Aug. 12, 1978 preseason game.

Stingley's greatest regret was that he had not reached closure with Tatum over the hit that changed his life forever. Now they are both dead.

"There was no penalty called on that play, and there was a lot of controversy about it. The best thing that resulted from that play is that the game is changed in terms of how officiating is done and in terms of what they call excessive violence," Stingley said in an interview. "It has opened the game up to allow receivers to get down field. And it has made the game more exciting. I know that a lot of receivers today would not be able to get open to catch 100 balls a year, playing against the defenses we played against back in the day. The game is a lot safer now."

Reconciling his lifetime fate was no easy task for Stingley.

"I was at my peak and ready to take on the NFL at that time. You have to try to find a rhyme or reason when things like that happen," he once said. "It took me awhile to figure out why it happened and exorcise all the demons. You try to get an understanding based on your knowledge or your feel of circumstances. All I had to do was come out of the house or travel around the country. Everybody I came in contact with let me know that there was more of a purpose for me in life than looking at it negatively. So I decided to look at it in a positive way."

Stingley formed his own foundation in 1993 to try to help give direction to youngsters growing up on the West Side of Chicago.

"Our young people are really getting away from us," Stingley said then. "I always believe that a more informed kid makes a better decision. I was born and raised in the same part of the city. I call it saving the lives of our youth, making a difference."

While Stingley remained bound to a wheelchair, Tatum battled the effects of diabetes.

It seems that practically the only way to get disability today from the league is by being in a wheelchair.

Tatum wrote a book shortly after his devastating hit on Stingley called "They Call Me The Assassin." On Aug. 12, 2003 – the 25th anniversary of the injurious hit – television producers attempted to get Stingley and Tatum together on the air.

"I was contacted by HBO because they were interested in getting me on their show," Stingley said that year. "Every time people in the media brought that up, it kind of took me back to that period of time of what happened and what I went through mentally and physically. And what my family went through. So it was kind of a tough year. I just felt like I had enough of talking about the injury, and the fact that (Tatum) never really talked to us (to apologize)."

Stingley was the true victim in the 1976 incident and was willing to talk one-on-one to Tatum. But he would not be exploited.

Still, it is my opinion that changing too many rules would make the game less appealing to the general public. They might as well go back to leather helmets and soft shoulder pads if they really want to make the game really safe. But who would want to pay to see that? A great part of the allure of the game of football, especially pro football, is that people want to see the hard hit, the jarring tackle. It's almost the same mentality as to why so many people like to watch auto racing or a bullfight. They are waiting to see a crash or an accident. They are hoping to see the possibility of someone getting hurt, or at the very least shaken up, let's face it. That element of danger excites everyone – same as in pro football. When 250- to 350-pound men collide on the football field, often at high speeds, something has to give.

Injuries are a necessary evil with this game that millions of Americans love and pay dearly to watch in person or on television. Not everyone is willing or able to take the kinds of risks pro football players take on every down. Yes, the money players make today is extraordinary, but that is not the only reason they play. They love the game; they love the action, excitement and competition that gets the adrenalin flowing. That is what makes the players special and unique. They are daredevils. Talented daredevils, but daredevils nonetheless.

The League is part of the determent as to what we are doing to our bodies and they are benefitting by what we are doing. As we get older, mentally and physically, we are past our prime as players whereas a normal person is in their prime, so it is impossible to compete. The League should share in the disability for the life of the player – and a wheelchair should not be the only criteria.

Losing A Friend 11

Dave Duerson, my friend and teammate from the 1985 Bears, took his own life in February 2011. I had seen Double D about three months earlier when we all celebrated the 25-year reunion of the '85 Bears through a number of events. I saw no indication from him at that time that he would consider taking his own life. I knew he had been going through some tough times financially with his businesses and his divorce. But I thought he had made it through that storm and was looking to start a new life for himself down in Miami.

Duerson said in his note that his final wish before committing suicide was that his brain be studied for indications that injuries from his playing career caused the mental health challenges he apparently had later in life.

The body of David Duerson was found on his bed with the sheet pulled up to the neck, according to the report following his death. "As the sheet was pulled off the body, a .38 Special revolver was seen next to the left hand with four intact rounds and one spent round in the five-shot cylinder."

Serving as a pallbearer for my Chicago Bears teammate and friend Dave Duerson left me feeling numb and sad. There were so many unanswered questions. Dave had been such a leader on and off the field, and it pains me that his life ended so soon. (Photo Courtesy of AP Images)

The report also noted that Duerson seemed to have methodically arranged his belongings before killing himself.

Multiple documents had been laid out on the dining room table, according to the report. "Multiple documents are laid out on the bed in the second bedroom, along with two framed certificates, framed medals and a folded American flag at the head of the bed... . The walk-in closet in the master bedroom has a football statute, three helmets from different football teams, and three football trophies."

I have agreed to sign up for the brain study sanctioned by the NFL through the Center for the Study of Traumatic Encephalopathy (CSTE) at Boston University School of Medicine.

Thirteen of the 14 deceased NFL players who were examined for the disease by the Boston University researchers have been found to have C.T.E., although there may have been accompanying factors tied to the disease, such as drug abuse, suicide or mental disorders.

C.T.E. stands for Chronic Traumatic Encephalopathy, which is a degenerative brain disease. For individuals who have a history of multiple concussions, the disease can only be diagnosed after a person dies. While the disease has gained tremendous attention with regard to former professional football players, C.T.E. also has been found to be prevalent among former boxers, hockey players and other participants of contact sports. Additionally, sports such as soccer, not generally regarded as a contact sport, have had an increase in participants suffering multiple concussions and other head injuries.

Common symptoms of the disease include short-term memory loss and other forms of dementia.

Duerson's family filed a wrongful death lawsuit in 2012, alleging that the NFL knowingly concealed information from its players regarding concussion

New Year's Eve 1986 was a memorable time on and off the field. Here Bears teammates Dave Duerson (L.) and Otis Wilson (silly hat) celebrate along with Alicia Duerson.

studies and information. The suit identified six other former NFL players who had committed suicide after suffering concussions as players.

The Duerson suit was filed separately from one filed by 126 former NFL players, including 15 past members of the Washington Redskins. Meanwhile, the NFL was attempting to have Duerson s lawsuit to be lumped in with the other NFL litigation in order to simplify the legal process for the league.

It is unfortunate that the lives of former players and their families have come to this. Pro football is a game, a business, a form of entertainment and a way of life for so many Americans. All wrapped up into one.

In 2012, another prominent player took his own life- linebacker Junior Seau. One of the game's most athletic and talented linebackers out of USC enjoyed a long career after being drafted No. 5 overall by the San Diego Chargers.

I hope the families of these deceased players are able to gain some sense of closure and resolution for what these men went through for years on the playing field. It is not an easy issue to resolve. We all love the game of football.

McMahon said that he was experiencing short-term memory loss and was concerned about the long-range effect of the numerous concussions he had suffered as a player. McMahon said he occasionally would go into a room in his house and forget why he went there. McMahon also agreed to participate in the Boston University brain study.

McMahon always has taken a lot of criticism for not being physically available to play in key games for the Bears after the 85 season. Many people point to that as being the No. 1 reason we did not win multiple Super Bowl titles. Yet I can remember seeing the physical beating McMahon took and how tough he was to endure what he did.

For instance, I believe he played with a broken hand for six games in 1984. Back then, the trainers and medical personnel would just shoot it up with a pain-killer, and you go play.

McMahon appeared at a news conference held by the Sports Legacy Institute in Dallas in early 2011, when he was helping to promote concussion education. The institute was hoping cities – including Dallas – would pass ordinances mandating strict concussion response and management for youth sports.

McMahon said he knows of five concussions he got as an NFL player. He also said there were times he played in games but could not remember what happened until he watched film a day later.

One thing is quite clear to me regarding concussions. Nowadays, there is so much more information available to the players. The casual, light-hearted approach that many of us took when somebody got his bell rung back in the 80s or earlier years is no longer acceptable.

In 2010, Indianapolis Colts receiver Austin Collie had to leave three games because of concussions. When he was interviewed on KHTK Radio, Collie said, "I think I have kind of put that behind me. I don't like to dwell on it too much just because it can affect your play going across the middle and catching another ball. You don't want things like that popping up in the back of your mind."

Collie said he didn't want to watch replays of the incidents in which he got hit and suffered a concussion.

"People want to show me or want to ask how I felt during that time," he said. "I just kind of brush it aside because it is one of those things that it is in the past and it's unfortunate. I was unlucky, but I'm just looking forward to this next season and getting on with it."

"I've known players who play with nine or ten concussions and who have lived on to have successful careers and haven't had any symptoms later on in life, so again everyone is different," Collie said. "Everyone handles each injury different and hopefully down the road it'll be perfectly fine."

Of course, ignoring concussions is no longer the way to go. You have to be smart about it and listen to the medical advice of trainers and doctors. Nowadays, I see trainers on the sidelines hiding the helmet of a player who has suffered a concussion. The old macho approach by many players is to insist on going back on the field, defying the advice of coaches and medical personnel.

I feel it is crucial that parents become involved in the decisions of their youngsters when it comes to deciding to play football in grade school and high school. I know that different states are taking a more pro-active role when it comes to informing families about the inherent risks of suffering concussions while playing football.

In the state of Illinois, for instance, Republican State Representative Tom Cross and the Illinois House of Representatives voted unanimously (112-0) on the passage of House Bill 200: Concussion Education Bill.

"This legislation is the direct result of concerns and ideas brought to me by parents and school officials in my district. Our children's safety depends upon everyone involved in school sports understanding how to spot a potential head injury and how to prevent the most serious consequences," Cross said in a press release.

There is no doubt that the tragedies associated with concussions have spurred discussion and positive activity to better diagnose and treat the symptoms.

In fact, on May 22, 2011, just months after Duerson's death, a special event took place in Richmond, Indiana. A panel discussion focused on head injuries.

The event was a fund-raiser for Wernle Youth & Family Treatment Center in Richmond, Ind., which is led by former Notre Dame football player Darrell "Flash" Gordon.

Before deciding to take his life, Duerson had agreed to lead the annual fund-raising golf tournament for Wernle, which is a residential facility for abused, neglected and severely challenged boys.

Duerson was from Muncie, Indiana, about 35 miles from Richmond, and played there many times as a young baseball and football player. Duerson also was inducted in the Indiana Football Hall of Fame, which is in Richmond.

Panelists for the discussion on concussions were scheduled to be Allen Pinkett, who starred at Notre Dame and in the NFL and now is a radio announcer for the Irish, Indianapolis Colts team physician Henry Feuer, and Alicia Duerson, who was married to Dave Duerson for 26 years.

Feuer has served on the NFL Committee on Concussions. The panel also included former NFL players Paul Flatley and Vagas Ferguson, plus Richard Bryant, president of the Indiana Football Hall of Fame.

The moderator was Dr. Brad Barrett from General Surgeons Inc. in Richmond. Barrett worked as a student trainer for Notre Dame when Duerson played there.

Sources told the *Chicago Tribune* that a private memorial service honoring Duerson was held in the locker room at Notre Dame Stadium.

Approximately 40 people attended the private service in South Bend, Indiana, conducted by Father Paul Doyle and school president Rev. John Jenkins. More than a dozen of Duerson's former Notre Dame teammates attended, including Allen Pinkett, Jon Autry, Joe Johnson, Chris Stone, John Mosley, Greg Bell and others, sharing emotional remembrances of Duerson during the 20-minute service.

After the service, everyone went through the tunnel and out onto the playing field before joining in the singing of the Notre Dame fight song. It was announced that a tree would be planted and a plaque dedicated to Duerson near the stadium.

Duerson was a two-time All-American and captain at Notre Dame before earning Super Bowl rings with the Bears and Giants as a 4-time Pro Bowl safety.

Eddie Payton, the older brother of the late Walter Payton, told the *Chicago Tribune* that Duerson's daughter would be awarded a college scholarship through the Walter Payton Scholarship Foundation.

Duerson left four children, the youngest of whom is 15-year-old Taylor. He also is survived by three sons: Chase (27), Tregg (25) and Brock (21).

"Dave raised money for 11 of the 12 Walter Payton Scholarship classics we've had," said Eddie Payton, a former NFL kick returner who is a very successful golf coach at Jackson State University in Mississippi. "I mean, he and I have been friends since before I got out of the National Football League and after he got out of the league. We shared a lot of stuff with each other. When I saw that the Duerson family asked, in lieu of flowers, to send donations to a memorial scholarship fund for Taylor, we just decided to, out of respect for him and what he has meant to Walter s memory, and with us being able to have 30 kids in school, we are just going to award a scholarship to the daughter."

"I don't think anybody would have a problem with that. With Dave's help and support, we raised over $1 million and have 30 kids in school. So, I mean, it is just the right thing to do."

Duerson was the winner of the 1987 NFL Man of the Year Award, since renamed the Walter Payton Award.

"The more I find out, the harder and harder it is to believe," said Eddie Payton. "I just wondered what could get so bad that you can't reach out to people who love and care about you. To me, and I have never been in that position where I ever thought about taking my life; it just seems like such a permanent solution to a temporary problem. With all of the things they are doing with modern medicine and science and research if you can just hang in there. One thing I know is that he wasn't a quitter. I mean, he was the ultimate competitor at everything. He always wanted to be the best, and he gave his best. It's just hard for me to believe that he did that. Only God knows. You have to respect what he decided to do. I mean, he thought about it. It didn't just pop up. He thought about it and the fact that he left his brain to the NFLPA for research shows that he put some thought into it. It has been really sad."

Payton, who played for the Vikings, Browns, Chiefs and Lions, recalled the fun times he had with Duerson, who wore jersey No. 22. Payton led the NFL with 53 kickoff returns for 1,184 yards in 1980. On Dec. 17, 1977, Payton returned a kickoff and a punt return for a touchdown for the Lions in a game against the Vikings.

"I wore No. 22 in high school and college and didn't get a new number until the pros," said Payton. "We talked about the double deuces and double Ds and the great guys who had worn the number before. We just had fun."

Similar to so many others who were confused by Duerson's decision, Payton recalled how upbeat Duerson seemed when they were together in 2010.

"He was at the Walter Payton Scholarship Fund golf tournament at the end of August in Jackson, Miss., and we had a good time. Then I talked to him again, it must have been October, because he was talking about getting married. He introduced his fiance (Antoinette Sykes), and he was talking about getting married. I told him, "Whenever you decide to do that, let me know. I will be there not only to support you, but to make sure you're not BS-ing us.""

Payton said he feels privileged to be able to assist the Duerson family with a scholarship for Taylor.

"There is no greater way to honor one of Walter's friends and Walter's memory than to educate his daughter," he said.

I was also saddened to learn of the passing of Hall of Fame tight end John Mackey in July 2011. In addition to being an exceptional pioneer of the game as the second tight end inducted into the Pro Hall of Fame, Mackey was an inspiration to all of us as the president of the National Football League Players Association.

Mackey suffered from dementia for many years before passing away at the age of 69.

He was the second overall pick of the 1963 draft and immediately made his presence known as a tight end, averaging more than 20 yards per catch as a rookie, catching passes from the great Johnny Unitas.

Due to dementia, Mackey spent the final years of his life in an assisted living facility. He was the inspiration behind The 88 Plan created by the league and the NFLPA in honor of Mackey's number. It provides $88,000 a year for nursing home care and up to $50,000 annually for adult day care for former players in need.

The NFL or union needs to provide players with health insurance for life. It's outrageous that after retiring you lose your health insurance.

From the time I played in high school and then at Tennessee State University and the NFL, I was taught to play with a sort of cautious abandon. You had to know the limits of your body and try your best to be the aggressor and not put yourself in needless jeopardy. Coach Joe Gilliam Sr., who was the defensive coordinator when I was there and later became the head coach at Tennessee State, is the person I tabbed to present me for induction in the Pro Football Hall of Fame during ceremonies in Canton, Ohio. He sent 140 guys into the NFL over his career. He taught me so much and showed me how I could push myself to be the best I could be.

By the time I reached the NFL, it was Buddy Ryan who took the handcuffs off me, so to speak, and showed me the way to play with reckless abandon, yet not without caution and purpose. I felt like I was one of the guys who helped change the game of pro football when it came to taking the ball from the quarterback.

I was very thirsty to make the Hall of Fame, even though as a child I never thought about that. I just wanted to play the game and have fun. I don't necessarily understand the process of making the Pro Football Hall of Fame. The numbers I racked up during my playing career have not changed since I retired. And the fact that the members of the Selection Committee never revealed how they voted from year-to-year continues to baffle me.

Make no mistake, I am pleased and honored to finally be in the house, as some of my Hall of Fame friends referred to it when I got the call. But I am perplexed when it comes to understanding the criteria that is used to determine who makes it in and who doesn't.

Quite significantly, I paid a stiff physical price for my many years of playing professional football, specifically in terms of numerous concussions that have resulted in my short-term memory loss issues and other injuries that cause me daily pain.

Hunter Hillenmeyer, who played linebacker for the Bears from 2003-2010, had his career curtailed by multiple concussions. He was placed on the season-ending injury reserve list after sustaining a concussion against Detroit in the first game of the 2010 season.

He remains deeply committed to educating young athletes and their parents about the perils of concussions in football and other contact sports.

Here's what Hillenmeyer had to say to the *Chicago Tribune* about his ongoing efforts: "We are trying to get up to a million young athletes base-line tested. So the hardest part now is getting schools signed up to get free testing.

"The Chicago Bears were one of the first teams to adopt it. Baseline testing had just been mandated six or seven years ago and now this is something that is offered to the masses. I think that is great of them to make that conscious effort, because one of the things that I have always spoken about is that it is great that we have made all of these improvements in terms of how it is handled at the NFL level. That will help protect their 1,800 players. But I think the more important thing is the carryover that it will have as far as how things are treated at the college, the high school and the youth levels."

Of course the NFL is not the only high-profile sport that is bringing increased awareness to the effects of head injuries. The National Hockey League, for instance, endured one of its most tragic off-seasons between the 2011 and 2012 seasons.

The NHL was stunned to learn of the suicides and/or accidental deaths of Wade Belak, Rick Rypien and Derek Boogaard. Meanwhile, questions lingered as far as the impact their head injuries might have had on their early deaths.

The Chicago Concussion Coalition conducted concussion training at Francis Parkman Elementary School in 2011.

The symposium was designed for Chicago Public School coaches, athletic directors and trainers as well as medical professionals and parents. Chris Nowinski of the Sports Legacy Institute, Alicia and Tregg Duerson, Mike Ditka, the Illinois Eye Institute, Access Community Health Network and the Department of Orthopedics and Division of Sports Medicine at Rush University Medical Center also took part.

"There can be nothing more important for a parent than to make sure that the coaches and people involved in sports understand the seriousness of brain injuries or concussions," Alexander Tennant of the coalition said. "You can recover from a concussion if you get the right kind of treatment. And you can prevent concussions by doing things to make the game safer."

I guess I am greedy when it comes to wanting the NFL to continue to have its fan appeal by being a violent, unpredictable sport. But at the same time, I would advocate for the safety of the players – both long-term and short-term. When I think about the pioneers of the game who sacrificed before me, I want the best for all concerned.

Another former Bears teammate of mine who died way too young was Todd Bell. He was a terrific safety and a good friend that I really could identify with in terms of his background and personality.

Todd died on March 16, 2005, of a heart attack at the age of 46 while driving his car in Reynoldsburg, Ohio, just outside of Columbus, where he had starred at Ohio State. Bell was a fourth-round draft pick of the Bears in 1981. He had replaced Doug Plank at safety, and Buddy Ryan loved him. Todd was a laid-back guy with a great personality. I wish I had been able to play with him more years with the Bears.

He was a very physical and dedicated ballplayer. He could play safety like a linebacker, yet he possessed the skills of a traditional safety, as well. Bell and Al Harris sat out our Super Bowl championship season because of a contract dispute. I wish we could have won another championship for Todd and Al's sake. Dave Duerson ended up replacing Todd with the Bears at safety.

Bell signed as a free agent to play for the Philadelphia Eagles in 1988 and '89. Sadly, he broke his leg as a member of the Eagles when he played against our Bears on Monday Night Football in 1989. That injury would serve to end his playing career prematurely.

One especially fun memory of Todd always will stick with me. On my way to team practices in Lake Forest, Illinois, I would always come to a certain spot where I would see Todd driving his really old Cutlass. He would see me and then really floor it. All of the old corrosion, clouds of dust and exhaust fumes would start coming from that car. I used to give him hell about that.

Bell remained connected to his alma mater following his NFL playing days. He had been named coordinator of the Minority Continuing Education Opportunities Program at Ohio State in 1997. Following his death, the center where he worked was renamed in his honor: The Todd Anthony Bell National Resource Center on the African-American Male.

I remember Todd as being a really sharp dresser who went out of his way to welcome me to the Bears in 1983. I appreciated the opportunity to get to know him and the fact that he always encouraged me along the way. Just think of the incredible nicknames of the NFL players in the 50s and 60s who defined the toughness of the sport.

Here are many of my all-time favorite nicknames: Fred "The Hammer" Williamson; Johnny "Blood" McNally; L.G. "Long Gone" Dupree; Alan "The Horse" Ameche; Eugene "Big Daddy" Lipscomb; Billy "White Shoes" Johnson; Madison Monroe "Buzz" Nutter; Dick "Night Train" Lane; Lou "The Toe" Groza; Norm "The Flying Dutchman" Van Brocklin; Ken "The Snake" Stabler; "Broadway Joe" Namath; Lawrence "L.T." Taylor; "Mean" Joe Greene; Ed "The Claw" Sprinkle; Flozell "The Hotel" Adams; Deion "Prime Time" Sanders; Tom "The Bomb" Tracy; "Slingin" Sammy Baugh; Howard "Hopalong" Cassady; Harold "Red'" Grange (aka "The Galloping Ghost"); Walter "Sweetness" Payton; Clyde "Bulldog" Turner; Bronislau "Bronko" Nagurski; Earl "Curly" Lambeau; Ted "The Stork" Hendricks; Hugh "The King" McElhenny; Earl "Greasy" Neale; Elroy "Crazy Legs" Hirsch; David "Deacon" Jones; "Deacon" Dan Towler; Joe "The Jet" Perry; Les "Two Ton" Bingaman and Ed "Too Tall" Jones and Claude "The Claw" Humphrey.

And, of course, I hope football fans will forever remember me: Richard "The Sackman" Dent.

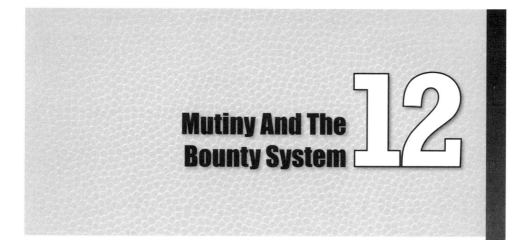

Mutiny And The Bounty System 12

The game of football always has been about beating the man in front of you, and in the case of professional football, keying on the superstars to make sure they don't beat you with one of their signature plays is crucial. On many occasions, opposing players would tell me that they tried to concentrate on limiting what Walter Payton could do on the Bears offense and what I could do on defense.

I took that as a compliment, and not as an indictment of their intentions to purposely injure me.

Much has been said and written about the New Orleans Saints, who were fined heavily and handed numerous suspensions in 2012, when it came to light that they had devised an intricate bounty system that paid players for injuring key opponents.

Saints coach Sean Payton was suspended for the entire season by commissioner Roger Goodell. Former Saints defensive coordinator Gregg Williams was suspended indefinitely. New Orleans general manager Mickey Loomis received an 8-game suspension, and the Saints were fined $500,000 and lost second-round draft picks in 2012 and 2013. Assistant head coach Joe Vitt was suspended six games.

Back in the 80s when I played with the Bears, we knew the Packers had bounties out for certain guys. When Charles Martin picked up Jim McMahon and threw him to the ground after he had thrown a pass and the whistle blew, everyone could see that Martin had a towel tucked in his uniform that had the numbers of certain Bears players he was targeting to knock out of the game. He was going beyond the point of trying to hit a player hard. He was trying to injure players and ruin their careers.

If you are talking about improving player safety throughout the league, the commissioner has the right and responsibility to do something to regulate the game. But at the same time, it has to be understood that this is a collision sport where people are going to get hurt. Not everybody can play this game, especially at the professional level.

Look at the sports such as boxing, kick boxing and mixed martial arts. People enjoy watching those sports, even though there is a high incidence of brutality and injury involved. And those methods used to inflict pain are calculated and measured. So there is a fine line in all of these sports when it comes to not injuring your opponent. Boxing has been around for decades. And if people expect football to continue as the game they have always known it, well, it is what it is.

If a player can't handle the rigors of the game, and can't take it, try something else. If you have a guy who is 6-5, 250, and he is running full steam before he hits a ballcarrier or receiver, injuries might happen. I don't care how much modern-day equipment you are wearing or what safety rules are being enforced. Hits happen!

Now, I can understand some of the newer safety rules implemented, such as the no-horse-collar rule for tackling. But sometimes, that's all a defender can do to bring a runner or receiver down. So in that case you are penalizing a guy for tackling a player who is trying to run for a touchdown. A defender is getting penalized for being fast enough to catch up with an offensive player and grab the back of his jersey. Now the officials are making a defender make a decision within a split-second on how to bring this runner down. That's pretty tough.

Some of these new rules make sense, but other rules seem to be trying to change the game from the way we have known it for decades.

People pay to see three things: the ball in the air, the quarterback down, and the ball in the end zone. If you get rid of that, then you will get rid of the fans. You can see that in the Pro Bowl game when defensive linemen are not trying to rush the quarterback ... it's a waste. People don't want to see that. At some point you have to put on a show.

There should be schemes to handle opposing players – whether it is a double-team or another specific tactic. That's all fair game. But getting paid additional money to injure an opponent should not be part of the game. We are all out there trying to make a living.

Buddy Ryan's 46 Defense was named after Bears safety Doug Plank, who finished his career in Chicago the year before I arrived. He talked about Ryan's mission to have our defense swarm and blitz and frustrate the offense during an interview with the *Chicago Tribune*.

"I've heard about bounties, having gone through the National Football League," said Plank, now head coach of the Philadelphia Soul of the Arena Football League.

I concur that even after Plank left the Bears, there was a certain mentality, attitude and determination with our defensive unit that did not need any financial motivation or encouragement to get the job done. Aside from the lingering effects of concussions, I worry about other ailments plaguing my former teammates.

William Perry was hospitalized in serious condition three years ago at the Aiken (S.C.) Regional Medical Center after suffering the effects of Guillain-Barre' syndrome, which was diagnosed the previous summer.

The disease is an inflammatory disorder of the peripheral nerves of the brain and spinal cord. The symptoms include general weakness of the legs, arms, breathing muscles and face.

Fridge Perry once boxed 7-foot, 7-inch former NBA player Manute Bol in 2002. He participated in Nathan's Famous Fourth of July Hot Dog eating contest in 2003. Even though Fridge could put away the food, I heard he finished about 40 hot dogs shy of the winner.

He remains in my prayers as he battles the disease.

If I could take you inside the huddle or the meeting rooms or the locker rooms we had when I played for the Bears, you could get a better idea of how intense players and coaches become and how determined we all become to impose our will on the opposition.

Players and coaches curse and yell and talk to themselves, really getting revved up for the competition at hand.

It was said that we had a certain swagger as a Bears team, and certainly as a defensive unit under Buddy Ryan we were able to back up all of the talk. That swagger came from the confidence we had in ourselves, individually and collectively. We were making tackles and taking names – not money for a bounty system to purposely injure players.

There always has been such a fine line between wanting to intentionally injure your opponent, as opposed to merely doing your utmost to prevent him from accomplishing what he is trying to accomplish. We knew, for example, that if a team such as the Rams had a strong suit of running the football, then we tried to shut that down. If an opponent featured an elite, passing quarterback, obviously we did all we could within the rules to make his day miserable by pressuring him, or better yet, sacking him. That is what the game of football is all about.

I think fans would have to be naive to think that such a violent sport as football would be devoid of players seeking to do bodily harm to an opponent. From the time we are in grade school, coaches are imploring defensive players to stick your head into the chest of the opposing running backs. Or crush the quarterback.

Taking those terms literally could be dangerous if not criminal, and I think most players were able to make the distinction between literal and figurative implementation of those commands.

You have to understand the unique relationships developed between coaches and players from the time we first put on a football uniform to the time we get paid to demonstrate our skills in front of an audience of millions of fans at the stadium and folks watching on television.

Young players are trained to obey their coaches from an early age. In many cases, head coaches and their assistants represent father figures to players who don't have a biological father living with them in their home. That same relationship could carry over into college and maybe into the pros for athletes who are intent on pleasing their coach while making a great impression on their teammates as well.

There is a unique culture in all of pro sports with regard to that sense
of obedience and compliance, and football truly represents that way of
thinking. It is almost like a military atmosphere, in which athletes are
expected to follow orders from their superiors, regardless of the risk involved
or the ethics behind the command.

So often we hear in football that, "this is the way it always has been done,"
or, "this is the system that has been in place for years." So athletes are made to
feel that it is beyond their power to change the system.

Just take a look at the fans at an NFL game when the TV camera scans
the crowd. Many fans are proudly displaying signs that read "Kill the quarterback!" or "Destroy the Packers!" Many fans look intense and revved up as
they vicariously experience what the players are going through on the field.
I am certain that millions of fans watching the games on television in their
homes and in bars and restaurants across the country bring that same attitude
as game time approaches. The entire atmosphere seems to promote a sort
of sanctioned violence and intimidation that would get you arrested on the
street.

Some of the most intimidating fans in the NFL are in Oakland. Many of
the Raiders fans dress as if it is Halloween every day of the year, and there has
been a history of more violence in and around Oakland Coliseum than on the
football field.

When the opposing quarterback or key receiver or running back is
injured and lying helplessly on the field, many times the home fans will cheer
derisively as he limps to the sideline.

Should there be a monetary bounty placed on a player? No. Yet there
seems to be an implicit message that it is OK to win a game by any means

necessary. Pro football is a business, obviously, and the livelihood of players hinges on their ability to win games. Taking it a step further, the careers of coaches, general managers, scouts and other assistants also rely on their team winning on a consistent basis, making it to the playoffs and, hopefully, winning a Super Bowl.

I can only imagine the kind of pressure the coaches on the New Orleans Saints felt as they implemented and condoned a bounty system to injure opponents. I mean, consider that commissioner Roger Goodell had warned that organization in previous years to steer clear of just that thing. Yet the Saints ignored his directive and continued to sanction such a system.

Players always have had little side bets with each other regarding special plays that could be made, such as an interception or a sack or big play on offense. Nothing wrong with that, and it was all in the spirit of helping your team win by legitimate means.

People say that money is at the root of all evil. Yet it is difficult for me to fathom that players in today's NFL, who make many more millions of dollars than we did in the 80s, can be motivated by an extra $500 or $1,000 dollars to purposely injure an opponent. That kind of money is chump change for players today.

Don't get me wrong. Everybody loves more money, me included. But to me, there has to be something else driving you as a football player to be the very best you can at your position. Maybe you can call it a sort of pride or manly bravado that inspires you. Maybe it is a recollection of a humble upbringing that keeps you on your toes and primed to do your best.

Playing professional football is a rare privilege and players present and past should never forget that. There are millions of wannabe professional football players in the world who had their dreams dashed after perhaps playing in high school or college. And for those players who do earn the opportunity to play professionally, most often it is only for three or four years on average, and then it is over, it's time to join the real world. I was blessed to have played for as long as I did with the Bears, 49ers, Colts and Eagles. Fifteen years was a pretty good run for me, and I count my blessings that I was able to last that long and remain productive.

Even during my years with the Bears when I felt I was being grossly underpaid compared to the production I was providing on the field, never did I consider performing less than my best on the playing field. No one needed to dangle an extra $1,000 in my face to get me to chase down the quarterback and fling him to the ground.

Of course, defensive players are the ones most often accused of trying to injure players intentionally with late or illegal hits. But I remember how Walter Payton used to take a proactive approach as a ballcarrier. He would lower his shoulder and deliver the first blow to an approaching tackler or safety to gain an advantage. He was so strong and had such great balance and agility that he made it uncomfortable for defenders to make a tackle and inflict pain on him.

Payton missed just one game during his brilliant 13-year NFL career. I know there were days when he didn't feel the best, and lesser players might have chosen to sit out. But not Walter.

When I hear the humble yet enlightening stories of the pioneer players in the NFL, I know that it took more than money to get them to perform at the top of their game.

Back in 1965, Gale Sayers was the No. 4 overall pick in the draft by the Bears out of Kansas. He was known as the Kansas Comet, and he went on to become the youngest player ever to be inducted into the Pro Football Hall of Fame, at the age of 34.

Sayers, who once scored a record six touchdowns in one game against the San Francisco 49ers as a rookie, played for a salary of $25,000 that first year. That wasn't much money, even back then. That same year, the Bears also drafted another Hall of Famer, Dick Butkus, out of Illinois, in the first round. Both Sayers and Butkus were offered more money to play in the fledgling American Football League, but they decided to play with the more established NFL, even though Bears' coach and owner George Halas was known for being tight with his money when it came to paying players.

I loved hearing the story about how Halas was able to motivate Butkus before a game against the Detroit Lions. Halas didn't use any kind of bounty system or any other financial motivation.

Butkus, who was known as a bruising, violent tackler as a middle linebacker, also handled long-snapping duties on occasion for punts. I guess Butkus was warming up before the game against Detroit when Halas strolled over and said to Butkus, "Hey, did you hear what Ed Flanagan said about you?"

Flanagan was the Lions' center. Butkus looked up and said, "No, what did he say?" But Halas didn't answer and just walked away. Halas had successfully created a little tension, anger and motivation in Butkus without offering any extra money as an incentive. Talk about playing for the love of the game! In the end, that's what all of us do, whether we are being paid $25,000 or $25 million a year.

I mean, how many times do we look at the fact that the expected lifespan of an NFL player is at least 10 years shorter than that of the average man? Or how many times do we hear about former football players complaining about how many knee replacements or hip replacements they have had to endure? Yet, resoundingly, those very same players almost always say that they would do it all over again. That is the thrill of the game.

The thrill of the game back in the 1950s and 1960s for defensive players was the fact that there weren't nearly as many rules restricting what they could do back then. For example, defensive linemen such as the great Deacon Jones of the Rams were allowed to use the head-slap technique against offensive linemen as they rushed the quarterback. I have seen footage of Jones's patented method of slapping a lineman's head on one side and then darting past him on the other as he sacked the quarterback.

Another advantage I have seen on old NFL films for defensive players was the fact that officials seldom threw the penalty flag if a player was tackled three or four yards out of bounds. Clothesline tackles also were permitted back then, as well as hits on defenseless receivers coming across the middle.

The one player I heard about recently who said he would not again go through the rigors and injuries associated with football was Hall of Fame cornerback Lem Barney from the Detroit Lions.

Barney, 66, told the *Detroit Free Press:* "If I look at the game now and I look back on it retrospectively, if I had another choice, I'd never played the game, at all, in my life. Never. Never. From all-city, all-state, all-conference, All-American, seven times All-Pro, I'm in eight Hall of Fames, it wouldn't be. It would be golf or tennis. I'm serious. Very serious."

Barney was one of 106 retired NFL players who filed a class-action suit against the league in Philadelphia federal court in January, 2012, accusing the league of negligence when it came to treating and diagnosing head injuries. When you are playing defense, you want to punish your opponent because that is the nature of what you are trying to accomplish. Yes, you are trying to intimidate, you are trying to make it uncomfortable, you are trying to make the offensive players think twice about coming your way. There is nothing wrong with that defensive philosophy. Because, believe me, the other team is certainly going to try just about everything to get an advantage over you.

What a lot of people don't understand with regard to these so-called bounty situations is that there is so very little time to think about that during the course of a game. During the heat of battle, you are concerned about getting the play called in the huddle, recognizing the offensive set in front of you, trying to beat the man in front of you and reacting to the offensive play. There is no time to daydream about wanting to make a little extra money by injuring another player.

It s not about taking a player's career out.

When it comes to player safety and possible bounty systems, what people have to keep in mind is that not everybody is equipped to play this game of pro football. That is why some people can play Pee-wee football, or maybe high school or college. It's the same thing in boxing. Everybody can't box, but we enjoy boxing. The sport of boxing hasn't changed a lot over the decades in terms of safety. At some point, I think we have to accept the fact that violent sports such as football and boxing have an inherent danger associated with them. Participants are being paid quite well to pummel their opponent. Whether that money comes in the form of their salary from the team or something unethical on the side in a so-called bounty system, let's call it the way it should be called.

You can't re-train a football player not to be physical and aggressive. So where do we draw the line? As defensive players, they are not allowed now to hit the quarterback above the shoulders or below the knees, so what you are looking at is a small area in the mid-section. The defender is running full-steam, trying to shed a blocker to get to the quarterback. If he gets there before the quarterback releases the ball, he has a split-second to recognize what area of his body he can attack. And often we are talking about a moving target. That is asking an awful lot in a split-second.

It is interesting to me to view the hypocrisy involved in the marketing of the game of pro football. All of the highlights of the game show the violent hits made over the years. That is what attracts fans and makes them salivate. On the other hand, all we hear about nowadays is improving the safety of the game. Well, I'm not sure you can have it both ways. If the game becomes too safe, people will not want to pay to watch it. There has to be an element of danger and risk involved to make the sport unique.

The graphic and specific words used by the coaches on the Saints, particularly former defensive coordinator Gregg Williams, are difficult for the average person to hear. But playing football is not for people with queasy stomachs.

That is not to say that I am not concerned about my personal well-being in years to come. I saw what happened to John Mackey later in his life, suffering from dementia for several years before he passed away in his late 60s. What kind of issues will I suffer? I don't know. It scares me, I can't lie. I am 52 now, and sometimes my memory goes. It is more short-term memory loss now. Am I just getting old, or is it a form of something worse?

The hardest collision I ever incurred during my playing days was with Kansas City Chiefs running back Christian Okoye. He was running full-steam and I was coming at him straight-on with hips and ass directly lined up behind me. I hit him with the crown of my helmet right on the top of his helmet. I had never seen stars like that before. Somehow I stumbled back to my defensive huddle, but it seemed like an out-of-body experience for me. I had to have suffered a concussion at that point.

Years later I ran into Okoye off the field and confessed to him that I had never before been hit like that, even though I was the one who initiated the contact. Okoye, who was 6-1 and weighed about 260 pounds and was exceptionally fast, admitted to me that he had not been hit that hard before, either. He was nicknamed "The Nigerian Nightmare," and he earned that moniker when he and I collided. Regardless of how much better manufacturers say they are making helmets, there is nothing that can protect you fully when so much weight and speed clash.

On My Way To Canton 13

After the announcement in February of 2011 that I would be inducted into the Pro Football Hall of Fame, my life turned into quite a whirlwind. Even as a finalist for induction, the Bears allowed me to be the honorary captain for the NFC Championship game in January 2011 at Soldier Field when the Green Bay Packers defeated the Bears and went on to win the Super Bowl against the Pittsburgh Steelers.

I served two stints as a player with the Bears, recording 124.5 sacks for Chicago and 137.5 total, including my stops with three other teams. I had a career-best 17.5 sacks in 1984 and led the Bears in sacks eight times. I would say the Bears got their money's worth out of me.

As I waited to be rewarded with the Pro Football Hall of Fame election, I kept the faith that I would eventually be recognized.

I had done my work and it's in the books. When this league looks back, it always looks back at some of the greater teams. After winning Super Bowl XX, we had home-field advantage in the playoffs the next

The unveiling of my Hall of Fame bust in Canton, Ohio, brought out a flood of emotions for me. And I couldn't think of a better person to help me with that honor than Joe Gilliam, my former defensive coach at Tennessee State.

few years. I don't recall missing too many games. And no matter who we played, I think a priority for opposing teams was controlling me or Walter Payton. My fans and friends were disappointed about the delay in my election to the Hall of Fame. I know that I entertained people over time and I enjoyed entertaining them. I knew that at some point I would get to the Hall of Fame.

As I prepared to be enshrined, I loved every moment, and I appreciated the good wishes from friends and fans.

I like to think that my election to the Pro Football Hall of Fame came right on time. That is to say, I can truly appreciate the significance of what this honor means. I knew what I had done. But, the frustration and anticipation really mounted over the years among my fans and friends as they wondered if my induction would ever happen.

Eventually, of course, it did happen. I was one of seven former NFL players and pioneers selected in 2011 and the 27th member of the Bears organization to earn enshrinement, the most of any team in the NFL. I was to be inducted with running back Marshall Faulk, linebacker Chris Hanburger, linebacker Les Richter, filmmaker and founder of NFL Films, Ed Sabol, cornerback/kick returner Deion Sanders, and tight end Shannon Sharpe.

Humility does not get a player into the Hall of Fame, I have come to realize. You need someone to recognize what you have done and let the world know about it.

As I said, my quarterback sack total during my 12 years with the Bears was 124.5. I had a Chicago single-season record and career-high 17.5 sacks in 1984, my second season in the NFL. I recorded double-digit sack totals each season from 1984 to 1988. I totaled eight double-digit sack seasons as a Bear and led the team in sacks in eight seasons.

I finished my career with 137.5 sacks, tied for sixth all time with John Randle in NFL history behind only Bruce Smith (200), Reggie White (198), Kevin Greene (160), Chris Doleman (150.5,) and Michael Strahan (141.5). My defensive teammates on the Bears Super Bowl championship team – Dan Hampton and Mike Singletary – reached Hall of Fame status before me, and I believe both were worthy of that honor.

Dan was an exceptionally good player, but I think during the times we were playing in the league, people on the other teams said that the two Bears players they wanted to knock out of the game were me and Walter Payton. It's nice when your peers look at you that way.

Regarding the Pro Football Hall of Fame voting, I feel strongly that the voting process should not allow for total anonymity. And I believe that former NFL players should be on the selection committee along with the pro football writers. It bothers me that voters for the Hall of Fame are not held accountable publicly for their decisions. A player is more than the sum of his stats, and former players are usually aware of a Hall of Fame candidate's impact on the game.

In all humility, I felt I was a major part of the Bears for many years. I was not the *Chosen One* for the Bears to promote – nothing against the guys that I played with; it's not their fault. The organization was putting their money behind certain guys. I was a guy who came in the league as the 203rd overall draft pick and they already had first-round picks Hampton and Al Harris. If you come in and replace one of those high draft picks, then you are sort of disrupting the order of franchise management.

When I first got word that I had finally been selected for the Hall of Fame, two people I had hoped to hear congratulations from immediately were Mike Ditka and Buddy Ryan.

It was later revealed that Ryan was battling cancer. New York Jets coach Rex Ryan, who had been a ball boy with the Bears, said of his dad, Buddy: "He's 80 years old, but he's doing great. he's tougher than shit. He has had other things in his life. He overcame encephalitis. He's overcome cancer twice. He's tough."

Buddy Ryan coached in the NFL for three decades as head coach of the Eagles and Cardinals, defensive coordinator of the Bears, Vikings and Oilers, and linebackers coach of the Jets.

I wish Buddy Ryan the best in his health battles.

Between 1984 and 1985, I recorded 34.5 sacks. Other Hall of Fame defensive ends before I was selected include Doug Atkins, Elvin Bethea,

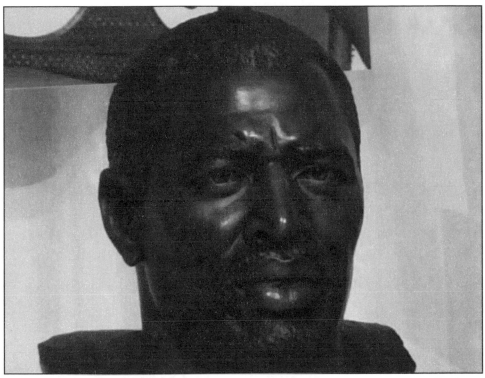

Being the first Pro Football Hall of Famer from Tennessee State means so much to me. I am not sure this bust looks like me exactly, but I accept it with great pride and humility. It will reside forever in the Hall of Fame Museum in Canton, Ohio.

Willie Davis, Carl Eller, Len Ford, Dan Hampton, Deacon Jones, Howie Long, Gino Marchetti, Andy Robustelli, Lee Roy Selmon, Reggie White, and Jack Youngblood.

There were players in the Hall of Fame before me who had nowhere close to the numbers I had. Every draft now, people start talking about, "Ah, they are looking for another Richard Dent." They are looking for another surprise long shot in the draft. Writers call me and ask me, "What about Mark Anderson when he was with the Bears?" Or, "What about this guy?" But when it is time to give me my due, nobody gives me my due. Finally, at last, I got my due with the Hall of Fame.

The Pro Football Hall of Fame organizers really know how to plan a week of celebration. Receiving the Hall of Fame sports coat, participating in the parade, being feted at dinners and, of course, enjoying the actual induction ceremony were all memories I will cherish forever.

I figured I did my thing during my playing days, and I don't take second to any defensive end who played the game, except for maybe Deacon Jones. Outside of him ... hell, I've got more interceptions than most linebackers. And I forced turnovers with forced fumbles more than probably anybody who has played the game. So I know what I have done.

Talking about Deacon Jones, I met him when he was receiving the Jake Gaither Award. We call it SWAK, and it is equal to the Heisman Trophy for black schools. Jones was the MC. In the lobby of the hotel, he had geri curls and was a doing a Miller Lite commercial at the time, "tastes great, less filling." I said, "Hi Mr. Jones, I am here to get the Jake Gaither." He said, "Oh, you are the defensive end. Why don't you come up to my room and I'll show you how to rush the passer, before you go out there and fuck it up." I said, "Oh, no, Mr. Jones, I'm from the school that had a lot of great defensive ends, Tennessee State." He just laughed.

The Bears always have been known for churning out stellar, Hall of Fame middle linebackers. Singletary became the 24th Bear enshrined during his induction in 1998.

Hampton was one of the keys on our 1985 defense that allowed just 198 points and shut out both playoff opponents before walloping the Patriots in the Superdome. In 1986, our Bears defense, guided by coordinator Vince Tobin, set an NFL scoring defense record (187 points allowed) for a 16-game schedule, a record that eventually was broken by the Super Bowl champion Baltimore Ravens.

I remember reading comments from Hampton as he awaited his selection for the Hall of Fame.

"I have always said that the awards meant nothing compared to the actual achievement and being a part of the team," Hampton said then.

"The fact that I was able to be on those great teams for those 12 years was enough, it really was. But you get around people like Ted Hendricks and Dick Butkus and Gale Sayers ... people who have had a huge influence on the game ... to be mentioned in that company is great."

Many observers felt the induction of former Oakland Raiders defensive lineman Howie Long the previous year enhanced the chances of Hampton making the Hall of Fame the next time around.

"You see guys who go in and you think: 'Maybe I've got a chance. Who knows?'" said Hampton. "If it happens, great. If it doesn't, the sun is going to come up tomorrow and I'll have another chance to play a round of golf. That's the way I look at it."

In 1985, our defensive front included Hampton, William "Refrigerator" Perry, Steve McMichael, and me.

During his 13-year NFL career, McMichael never missed a game; "He played in 191 games in a row. That Bears' franchise record was broken in 2010 by long-snapper Pat Mannelly.

"I have a greater appreciation, and people should have a greater appreciation of me because of how long I played the game. It's a yearlong job," McMichael has been quoted as saying. "You work out hard. You don't get all those little injuries. I think this is where these new kids are missing the boat. You want to relax and take it easy, but after you get out of the game and you look back on it, you say to yourself: 'Man, that happened so fast. Why didn't I do more?' You're going to look in the mirror one of these days and you aren't going to like the person you see in it."

By 1988, Al Harris started at left defensive end and Hampton moved inside to tackle. Hampton was able to practice just a few days a week at that point because so much of the cartilage had been surgically removed from his knees. But he contributed big plays on game day, often blocking extra points and field goals on special teams or deflecting passes at the line of scrimmage. He wound up his career in 1990, having played 157 games.

I will always remember McMichael as a rock-solid, intimidating player and eccentric personality. He always kept us loose. I remember McMichael always talking about how difficult it was at first for him to impress Ryan.

New England had cut McMichael after drafting him out of Texas.

"Nobody has ever seen me in a New England Patriots uniform," McMichael said. "There is a picture of me in one in the books. New England labeled me the criminal element in the league. You know, how I was in practice. They had heard the stories about me running around in the combat zone in Boston, and they knew there were some practices where I didn't get any sleep the night before. So they called me up to the office and said, 'We're releasing you because we think you are the criminal element of the league.' But it was not a bad thing, because then I came to the Bears."

It was six weeks into the season when the Bears called him up to replace an injured defensive lineman. Well, veteran Alan Page never practiced much with the Bears toward the end of his career. So Mongo, as we called McMichael, realized that first day that he was going to have to handle every play of that practice. Before the practice started, Buddy Ryan came up to him and said, "Hey, No. 76, we're going to work your butt off today. Have you been staying in shape?"

My Hall of Fame induction week was made even more memorable because a long-term collective bargaining agreement was finally reached. In this photo, NFL commissioner Roger Goodell and players association president DeMaurice Smith shake hands after signing the papers in front of the Hall of Fame Museum.

Mongo said, "Yeah, I've got this big black Great Dane. And me and him have been jogging." After practice McMichael was bent over and gassed after wind sprints. And we all could hear Ryan coming up from behind him saying, "Shoot, No. 76, we should have signed the dog."

Hampton wondered before his selection if the fact there were so many outstanding Bears defensive players might hurt the chances of more individuals making the Hall of Fame.

"All I see is all of these Steelers (five defensive players from the Super Bowl championship Pittsburgh teams of the 1970s) who keep getting in. And you look at the stats and our defenses were, I think, quite a bit more effective than they were. Winning Super Bowls has a huge bearing on who goes in the Hall of Fame. I think that's unfortunate," said Hampton.

Buddy Ryan introduced the revolutionary 46 defense that became the dominant scheme in the mid-1980s. He called it the 46 defense in respect to former hard-hitting Bears safety Doug Plank, who moved into an outside linebacker's position on occasion. Singletary felt the effectiveness of those Bears defenses has been understated because we made it to only one Super Bowl.

"It's unfortunate. I heard a commentator say recently that the '46 defense was unconventional and that there was just a short stretch that it was effective. Give us the credit we are due. We won football games week in and week out. We had so many players banged up down the stretch, like (quarterback) Jim McMahon, that we just didn't have it" (an offensive threat). I agree with that assessment.

When Hampton first became a candidate for the Hall of Fame, the modern-era finalists were determined by a vote of the Hall of Fame's 38-member Board of Selectors from a preliminary group of 71 players, coaches, and contributors.

The Board of Selectors meets annually at the time of the Super Bowl to elect new members. There is no set number for any class of enshrinees, but the board's current ground rules stipulate that between four and seven new members will be selected each year. The 1973 and 1976 classes of three were the smallest ever named.

Every candidate must receive at least 80 percent approval of the board at the annual meeting before he can be elected.

One especially vociferous member of our 2011 Pro Football Hall of Fame induction class was former tight end Shannon Sharpe, who also grew up poor in Georgia. Shannon and his older brother, Sterling Sharpe, were raised by their grandmother in tiny Glennville, Ga. "It's not an accident that two brothers came from that environment and became successful in the National Football League. That is not coincidence," Sharpe said at the Hall of Fame induction luncheon. Sharpe helped develope off-season training with me and Drew Hill.

And Hampton, of course, was correct.

On the other hand, my wait for the call to the Hall of Fame seemed endless.

I keep coming back to the fact that I felt as if I was taken lightly, so to speak, when it came to being publicly praised and promoted by the Bears organization, and I felt that it adversely affected my bid to be selected for the Pro Football Hall of Fame.

I am proud to say that during the 75-year anniversary of the Bears franchise, I was named as one of the Bears' all-time first-team performers by at least one publication.

Many other outstanding Bears players have emerged since then, but I like to think I would remain a starter.

The Bears have more players in the Pro Football Hall of Fame than any other NFL club, making the selection of an all-time Bears defensive team that much more difficult.

There have been over 200 NFL inductees enshrined since the Hall of Fame opened in Canton, Ohio, in 1963.

The Bears have played more than 1,000 games in franchise history. George S. Halas, the team's founder and head coach for 40 years, won 324 games, an NFL record until it was surpassed by Miami Dolphins coach Don Shula.

During the 1940s, Halas' Bears won four straight conference titles and three world championships. They outscored their opponents 2,164 to 842 during that span, compiling a record of 62-7-1. In 1963, Halas coached the Bears to a title, a 14-10 win over the New York Giants at Soldier Field.

But it was during the Ditka years from 1982-92 that the Bears gained international acclaim following their lopsided win in Super Bowl XX.

"During the Ditka years, we were the best-known team in the world," the late Ed McCaskey once said. He was Halas' son-in-law and the Bears chairman of the board. "But the Bears or any other team will never approach the era of Halas, (Art) Rooney and (Wellington) Mara and George Marshall. They ran the show. Now, every team is one voice."

RICHARD DENT'S HALL OF FAME SPEECH

Pro Football Hall of Fame Field at Fawcett Stadium
August 6, 2011

"Thank you, thank you, thank you. You know, I grew up in a time where a man always said, 'I have a dream,' and that man was Martin Luther King. And as a kid growing up at that time listening to him, all I could do is dream. I wanted to be someone special that my mother and my father and my family looked up to. I wanted to be someone that, you know, I enjoyed playing a game, but then again I enjoyed working and just trying to take care of myself.

"When you've got seven brothers and one sister and you're number six out of nine, there's not much left over for you. When you ask for food, my dad would tell you, 'a burger's only going to last for a second. You don't need anything. I don't have a dollar for you.'

"Richard Dent went to work and tried to find himself. It was tough. Not in my wildest dream that I thought I'd be here. When you have dreams, it's very tough to say that you can do everything by yourself. It's all about other people. None of us can get anywhere by ourselves.

"I had a friend of mine by the name of Scott Dean who gave up the band to help me to stay in school and helped me to pursue my dream. I had a young lady by the name of Ms. Sandy Payton. Ms. Payton and I used to hang out in her store when I was eight years old, and she decided to give me a job because she knew that I was taking things. It was a clothing store, so she taught me a lot about business, so she gave me something to look forward to.

"There was another lady by the name of Ms. Mary Knight. Ms. Knight's about 93 years old. Ms. Knight, you know, you took care of my mother. My mother and I and took care of people, raised people, raised people in our community, and I commend you so much, Ms. Knight, I appreciate your love. I appreciate you coming here to celebrate this with us.

"There is, also a guy by the name of William Lester that told my mother, 'Look, I'm going to try to do something for him.'

"When I grew up I used to watch Claude Humphrey, and I used to watch Tommy Nobis, and Hank Aaron, and Muhamad Ali, so as a kid, I loved Claude Humphrey and didn't know I was going to go to Tennessee State. I took a little piece of Claude, and little piece of Muhamad Ali and said, 'I am going to raise some hell.' So from there, William Lester, like coach said, he dropped me off. Tennessee State wanted three other friends of mine from Murphy High School. Murphy High School guys, would you stand up? Chuck, I appreciate you guys. You know, Coach Lester dropped me off and you know we finished school August 6. I was at Tennessee State August 8, and before you know it, I was working at Sunbeam Bread August 9th and in summer school.

"But, you know, that was important to me. It was important to me that William Lester and I moved out of the neighborhood, And Coach Lester gave me a ride for two years in a row. Between him and his wife, they gave me a ride and allowed me to walk about a mile home, but yet I didn't want to transfer. I came in the game late. And William Lester and his family, you know, he died a couple years ago.

"We had a chance to do this at the Georgia Hall of Fame, and I just want to say 'Thank you,' because if it weren't for him, I couldn't be here today. I wouldn't be in Chicago, and I'd have never gotten to Tennessee. So thank you there.

"Also, the first guy out of Atlanta, Georgia, out of Atlanta public school for the Hall of Fame, the first player out of the state, you know, I just couldn't believe it. What, 100 something years that one could do such a thing, but that's what took place.

"So my Tennessee State people, are you out there? I love you all, because my Tennessee State people shaped me, you know, loved me. I appreciate the band coming out, and it was nothing like going to big blue. Big Blue was awesome.

"All the guys that I played with there, I appreciate you guys coming out. Aron Ford, Joe Adams, John Smith, and if you don't mind, I would love for you guys to reach on out and give my coach, give your coach, you might have been a student or you might have been any alumni, I'd love for everybody to just stand and give Coach Gilliam a hand for all that he's done in the last 35 to 40 years. A man that sent numerous guys to the pros and had a 1948 undefeated team in Indiana.

"Let me tell you, you don't meet this kind of person too often. I used to hate this person, but I learned to love him (Coach Gilliam). You know what I mean? I learned to love him because he shaped me and he made things work for me. Coach, thank you, Coach. Thank you, thank you.

"Dr. Frederick Humphries, our former president, I'd like to say hello to you, doc. Thank you for coming out. Paula, our new president, thank you for bringing the band out. I know it cost you a lot. We are the first, and well, I should say I am the first for Tennessee State, and I really appreciate your love and I appreciate you coming out and bringing the kids out.

"Craig Gilliam is coach's son, and Craig is first guy that taught me how to break down films. Taught me how to, you know, snyc in on ballplayers. Craig, I'd like to say, 'Thanks,' and I appreciate your love. Thank you a lot, Craig. Thank you a lot, baby.

"There are two other guys that I should say, 'I stand on your shoulders,' and that's Claude Humphrey and "Too Tall" Jones. I think "Too Tall" is out here somewhere. "Too Tall" and Mr. Humphries, Claude Humphrey I want to say, 'Thank you,' because there wouldn't be no me without you.

"I used to get in a little trouble in college back in the day. And there was a gentleman by the name of Dean Murrell. Dean Murrell and Ms. Murrell were husband and wife, and they were the Dean of the school. Ms. Murrell, I want to say, 'Thank you.' Please stand, thank you, Ms. Murrell. Thank you for your time, for Dean who is not here anymore, but thank you.

"Also I'd like to say thanks to some guys that I started the game with, Jim Osborne and Emery Moorehead, and Neal Anderson, Al Fontenot. And I'd like to say, 'Thanks, I like that '85 team out there.' I know I've got that Chicago '85 team. Where you at? Please give me a little love. There they are. There they are, thank you. Gary Fencik, Tyrone Keys, Mike Richardson, Emery Moorehead, Dan Hampton, Steve McMichael, love you, Steve. Steve, I hope to see you up here some time. You were the heart of the defense, and you made it work for us.

"Most important of all, it's a guy by the name of Jimbo Covert that I had to line up and practice against day in and day out. He made the game easy for me, because I knew I wasn't going to face a guy like him in the game. But me and Jimbo, we definitely pushed each other to make each other the best. Walter was great for a long time. He led rushers for a long time. Jimbo, I look forward to seeing you on the stage. I love you brother, thank you.

"The guy that found me was a guy by the name of Bill Tobin. I was so skinny when I came in the league. I was 228 pounds. I had bad teeth and I didn't know what was going to take place. But, Bill, appreciate your love, Bill. Please stand. Thank you. Yeah, I know you wanted me to go higher, I went lower, but that's all right. We're here.

"Dale Haupt was our defensive line coach. Coach Haupt, thank you for coming and your family. Appreciate you. That's Mr. Drill Sergeant, guys, Mr. Drill Sergeant.

"John Levra, Coach Levra thank you for coming, too. Thank you a lot.

"Also, you know, I love to thank the Chicago fans and the people in Chicago. You know, it's such a great place to play. It's where the game started. There's not a better place to play. It means so much to me to get a chance to play there where a guy like Walter Payton, and a guy like Dick Butkus, and a broad shoulder like the city of Chicago. It was a pleasure to get a chance to entertain them on Sunday to allow us to come into their home and have so much fun.

"Thank the 49ers and the Eagles and the Colts also for giving me a chance to come and play with those folks.

"My dad, Dad, I know you're sitting there. Thank you, Dad, because you taught me some things about hard work. You know, I used to bump a lot of clothes with you and click a lot of clocks, and I'm just glad that you didn't allow me to go to jail with you that day when we went fishing and you didn't have a license anymore. The guy told you to follow him, and we went another route. Thank you, Dad, thank you, because I was seven and my brother was six. Who knows what was going to happen in Covington, Georgia, if you know Covington, Georgia, you know.

"Obviously, my mother was my heart. And I tell you, I couldn't be here without her. Everybody else were daddy's boys, I was mama's boy. I'm so thankful to be here. I wish my mother was here, but obviously not. My sister, Brenda, my brother Naji, and Johnny, and Steve, you know, thank you guys because you guys had that band back in the day.

"In the '60s, if you had a lot of kids, everybody wanted to be the next Michael Jackson group, and hell, it didn't happen, but I went and cut some grass.

"Brothers, thank you, guys. Thank you over there, my brothers. Thank you. Thank you a lot.

"You know, my two daughters, Mary, Sarah, I love you to death. My son, R.J., you guys got this legacy, and I look forward to you guys to take it on with the Make a Dent Foundation. Angie Sandborg who has been my mother in Chicago, thank you, Angie, for helping me out, because nobody can do anything alone. You have to have some type of support mechanism.

"When I tell kids, 'Don't look at me as a player. If you're going to think of me, you look at Mr. Dent. Now take D, the first letter in my last name, for dreaming, you must dream. You must dream and you must be dedicated to proceed with anything in life. Okay, when you dream, you have to get up and do something about it.

'The letter E, you have to be educated to figure out what to do, how to do and when to do. The letter N, you represent your name, your family, your team, where you came from, whoever. And the letter T is, you know, you're going to get knocked down one day, folks. But you got to get back up and you've got to try again.'

"These challenges were tough for me here today. I don't have a lot of time to tell you how long it took to get me here. But I took those four letters and I was destined to make something of myself, of my community, and my friends, and my loved ones, everybody to appreciate.

"I'd like to thank some people that are not here anymore that are important to my life also. Obviously my mother, Dwayne Roberts, Brian Howard, a buddy of mine named Bruce Walker who taught me the pass rush to move in Tennessee State. Steve Moore who I played against in the Super Bowl. We were both rookies coming out of it. And obviously a guy named Fred Washington, who was just at the Bears for a short time, who I came to love.

"A guy like Todd Bell, who both of us saw ourselves the same. Todd was a great man. Obviously, the late Dave Duerson and the late Drew Hill.

"But the guy who I tried to pattern myself on was the late great Walter Payton. Walter was the best of all. I loved watching this man go to work. Also I'd like to congratulate the class of 2011. Congratulations, brothers. I look forward to being in this house.

"As a kid, you look at some of these guys left to right, I've watched these guys as a little one and never thought everything in sports I'd dream and I'd seen myself accomplish, but I never thought about being in the Hall of Fame. This kid I had a chance to meet one time, and he told me, 'Hey, brother, keep doing what you're doing, you'll get there one day.' The leader just started.

"Also, I'd like to thank all the people at the Hall of Fame for the festivities, and putting this on. Like I told my friends last night, 'It's time to party. It's time to drop it like it's hot.'

"I have to thank my buddy, M.J., my buddy at Luke Capital, FirstEnergy and First Communications, and the Borris family for putting this party on the for us. Thank you all, love you all, see you down the road.

"I take tremendous pleasure in realizing that I have become the 27th member from the Chicago Bears' storied franchise to be enshrined in the Pro Football Hall of Fame in Canton, Ohio. When I think of the many famous names I have joined from the Bears, it boggles my mind. Names such as George Halas, Walter Payton, Gale Sayers, Dick Butkus, and on and on.

"Becoming a member of the Pro Football Hall of Fame is something that no one ever will be able to take away from me."

DeEtta first arrived in Illinois in May 2011. The HOF induction in Canton was August 2011. DeEtta and Shiloh were living in a house that she rented while she sorted things out in her head. She and I spent time together then, but she was still pretty stunned by the recent turn of events. Though she did help me plan for and also attended the HOF induction events with me, she asked that she and Shiloh not be mentioned in my speech. We both decided that our situation was a private family matter and that introducing Shiloh as my son on national television wasn't appropriate.

Though I don't believe in carrying regrets around with me, I had two leaving the stage that day. I forgot to thank Leslie, Mary and Sarah's mother, for the amazing job she did raising my daughters. And I regret that the circumstances at the time didn't allow me to acknowledge Shiloh as one of my beloved children.

Oh, What a Season: The '85 Bears
14

Many members of our 1985 Bears Super Bowl team were able to attend the 25th anniversary celebration of that accomplishment at the White House in 2012.

I was honored and pleased to attend after the invitation was extended by President Barack Obama.

Dan Hampton decided not to attend the celebration because he said he was told children and spouses were not invited, and also because he said he is not a fan of the President.

Hampton's decision was a personal one, yet it caused a bit of controversy, even among some of his former teammates.

Former Bears tight end Tim Wrightman posted the following message on his Facebook page to counter the position of Hampton:

"Why I'm going to the White House: Out of all the players from the '85 Bears arriving on October 7th, I would probably say I am the most conservative. I live in the reddest of red states (Idaho) and I make a living with guns, I am also not a fan of the policies of the current President; however, this is a celebration for the achievement of a great football team, not a political rally.

"I mean, did you really think it was appropriate for Marlon Brando to not accept the Oscar? I can differentiate between celebrating our team, the President and the Institution of the Presidency. Of course, I played on the smart side of the line of scrimmage. This is the Bears' once in a lifetime opportunity that has been given a second chance. Some people don't realize our initial trip in 1986 was cancelled because of the Challenger space shuttle accident. I think it was a classy thing for President Obama to right the misfortune of our team. Besides, the White House is not President Obama's house, it's the people's house.

"Some of my more notable teammates have stated various reasons they will not attend, and they have every right to have their own opinion and reasons for not going. 'I'm not going because they didn't invite our wives.' Well, would you take the wife you had when we won or the newest one? It was 25 years ago, let it go & will you stop doing car commercials that say you were a Super Bowl Champ? And so what if it was 25 years ago? If winning the Super Bowl is so easy, how come the Bears haven't won since?

"Further, I'm not so arrogant to think that by going to the White House people are going to believe I endorse the President. Nor do I believe my invitation will cause people to vote for President Obama just because I visited the White House. This is a great opportunity for me to see my fellow teammates one more time, and as a conservative I never take myself out of the game. I always want an opportunity to discuss and to debate my positions. You never know whose mind you might change and decisions you may influence. Being together as a team and a country is the only way we can get through our current predicament & GO BEARS!" – Tim Wrightman

A few years ago, our 1985 Bears were ranked as the second greatest Super Bowl team ever on the NFL Network's documentary series "America's Game: The Super Bowl Champions." We were ranked behind the undefeated '72 Dolphins. ESPN rated our '85 Bears as the greatest NFL team of all time.

I like to point out that the '72 Dolphins played an easier schedule than we did in 85. No opponents on the '72 Dolphins schedule made the playoffs, and nine of their 14 opponents finished with a sub-.500 record. Miami finished 17-0 with a 14-7 Super Bowl victory against the Washington Redskins.

Our '85 Bears were 18-1, including the postseason, and allowed the fewest points (198) in the NFL that year, as we did not permit our opponents to score more than 10 points in 11 of our 16 regular-season games. Offensively, our Bears scored 456 points, which was second in the league.

We were a brash collection of characters who dared tape a Super Bowl Shuffle video midway through the regular season.
Our championship season clearly was the culmination of a lot of pent-up emotions and reactions from our unrequited 1984 campaign.

When I think about the fabulous '85 season, I can't help but think about how the '84 season ended for us in the playoffs. We had finished the regular season with a 10-6 record and we were excited about our chances in the postseason, even though we lost our starting quarterback, Jim McMahon, to a kidney laceration during the 17-6 victory over the Raiders in early November of '84.

Before the playoffs started in '84, our team traveled to Sewanee, Georgia, to practice. We did not have an indoor facility back in Chicago at that point, so we needed some place warm to practice in late December.

I remember being excited about the chance to see my mother in Georgia during the time we were down there practicing for three or four days. Her birthday was on Christmas Eve, and I was determined to personally take her a present. Now, I had seen other Bears' players given permission to visit family or whatever when we would travel as a team for a road game. Some guys would even leave directly off the plane and head for their destination, without accompanying the team to the hotel.

So, I didn't think it would be a big deal for me to go home, see my folks, and then come back to go to work. On this occasion, we arrived at the Atlanta Falcons practice facility in Sewanee, which wasn't that far from my family's

One of the first things that stood out to me when I first joined the Bears was the enormous size of many of the players. Keith Van Horne, the Bears starting right tackle, stood 6-feet, 6 inches and weighed at least 265 pounds at the time. I knew as a rookie that I would have to put some weight on my skinny frame pretty quickly to stand up to these guys in practice. Our starting offensive line for seven years included Van Horne and Jim Covert at the tackles, Mark Bortz and Tom Thayer at the guards and Jay Hilgenberg at center.

home. It was probably a 20-minute drive. We lived in Stone Mountain at that time. I just wanted to get home to see my mom for a short period of time, to see the expression on her face when I gave her the gift.

By the time we got to the team hotel in Sewanee and got our food served, it was around 9 or 10 o'clock. I asked Coach Ditka for permission to go to the house and he said; "As long as you are back by 11."

Well, it's already 10 o'clock! I'm saying to him, "Dude, come on. You want me back at 11? So you want me to drive over there, drop the gift off, and turn around and come right back? The playoff game is four or five days away."

I didn't appreciate that, so I was a little pissed off. All of my teammates knew I was pissed off. So Mike Singletary, who was one of our captains, went over to talk to Ditka and plead my case. This time, Ditka said, "OK, as long as you are back here by 12."

At that time, it was damn near 11 o'clock when Ditka made his latest decision. So it still was only one hour for me to drive home, drop off the gift, and drive back to Sewanee. So now I am really pissed. Faced with this dilemma, my brothers came over to my hotel to visit me. As it all turned out, later in that week we ended up having a cookout at my house in Stone Mountain. I invited a bunch of teammates over – Tyrone Keys, Mike Richardson and a few others.

Anyway, the next day we have our regular team meeting and I noticed that Ditka seemed all uptight and upset when I walked into the room. I sat down and the first thing Ditka said was, "Are you happy now? Are you happy?"

I am looking around and I said, "Who are you talking to?"

Ditka said, "I'm talking to you. Are you happy?"

Then I said, "You know what. I should have just gone on home and not even bothered about asking you."

This is all happening before the meeting even starts, and he has a thorn in his ass about me for whatever reason. All I know is that if you talk to a person a certain way, without respect, you are going to get the same disrespectful response back at you. That's just the way I was brought up. I don't want to disrespect anybody, but don't disrespect me, either.

Then Ditka said, "You know, we're down here to play a game. Football comes first."

Then I said, "Well, my family comes first."

Ditka said, "Well, who pays you?"

I said, "The same person who pays you, pays me. That's who pays me."

Then Walter Payton starts screaming and he tells us to knock it off. So from that point the meeting sort of got going.

That was the type of in-house friction I had become accustomed to with the Bears. In many ways, I guess you could say we were a dysfunctional family. Here I am, a second-year guy who is just asking for the kind of permission that I see happening with other players, yet I wasn't getting that privilege. Here I was a Pro Bowl player, leading the league in sacks, and I am getting treated with little respect from my own coach and organization.

I had proven that I was a blue-chipper, even though I had been drafted in the eighth round. They didn' t have to smell the place up with their attitude.

With backup quarterback Steve Fuller leading the way, we had captured our divisional title and went on to defeat the Redskins, 23-19, in Washington's RFK Stadium in our first playoff encounter. Defensively, I felt like that was one of the most physical games we had played, and we just beat them down. I thought we had a hell of a game. I was being double-teamed, but I still made things happen. I was setting up on the inside in our 46 Defense, playing over the offensive guard, just as I had been set up to play in college. I was able to penetrate that gap as quickly as I could.

Everything clicked the way we thought it would against the Redskins. They were a good blocking group, but not great. Their philosophy was to protect the quarterback. If you couldn' t stop their running game, they would keep repeating those calls until you stopped it. But if you could get them out of their scheme and pattern, you could make some things happen defensively. That' s what we were able to do that day.

That Redskins game sort of reinforced within us how great of a team we could be. I remember Redskins running back Joe Washington trying to cut back on one particular play. We had our safety, Todd Bell, come down and hit him so incredibly hard. Washington hit the ground and jumped up, snapped his chin strap off and said, "Damn, you all are really hitting hard out here!"

Years later I saw Joe Washington at Walter Payton's funeral in 1999. Joe said to me, "Remember me saying that?"

I said, "Yeah, I remember that game and what you said on the field. I can never forget it."

That hard-fought victory over Washington set us up to face the San Francisco 49ers at Candlestick Park in the NFC Championship game. The winner, of course, would advance to the Super Bowl. We wound up feeling humiliated after losing 23-0 to San Francisco. We really missed having McMahon as our quarterback, even though Fuller filled in as best he could. Offensively, we just didn't click as well, because the 49ers were able to concentrate all of their defensive efforts on stopping Payton.

I just remember the feeling of personal frustration after that NFC Championship game loss in '84. It was only my second year in the NFL, yet I came so close to making it to the ultimate game – the Super Bowl. It was so close, yet so far from my grasp. The city of Chicago was hungry for a Super Bowl title, as well. The last time the Bears had battled in a championship game had been 1963, when they edged the New York Giants, 14-10, at Wrigley Field. The Super Bowl had not yet been invented then. It was simply called the NFL Championship Game. Still, the '63 Bears were considered world champs.

I had started the last 10 games of the '84 season and was really starting to establish myself around the league. Between 1984 and '85, I recorded 34.5 sacks.

So on the plane coming back from San Francisco, I remember all of us talking and saying that we were going to become committed to winning it all in 1985. And win it hands down.

From a personal, business standpoint, I wanted some sort of security for my contract. I wasn't necessarily asking for a new contract, even though I was way underpaid compared to my production. The year before, I just remember getting hurt and getting banged up so badly. Now, I was a Pro Bowl player making just 80 grand with a great future ahead of me. The Bears had two years plus an option contract on me. So I wanted to have the Bears sweeten the option part of the contract. The Bears said they didn't want to talk about that option year just yet. So I said they had to at least give me some large insurance policy.

At one point prior to the '85 season, the Bears sent player personnel director Bill Tobin down to Georgia to meet with me. It was at that point that he ticked me off by indicating I would have to wash cars or something like that to make a living if I didn't play football. "I said to Bill Tobin (following the car washing incident) – "get the hell out of my house. And my mom came in the room and Tobin asked her to help me make a good decision. She said, "he is a grown man and he can make his own mind up." So a day later the Bears agreed about the insurance policy and who did they have pick me up at the airport in Plattville, Bill Tobin, who apologized for what he had said and he told me that he was just following orders. Of course, I accepted his apology. I admire a man who apologizes when he knows he is wrong.

Once the contract situation was ironed out, I was able to concentrate on playing football and winning games. While I won the Super Bowl MVP trophy, there were a number of other awards given to my teammates.

Walter Payton won the NFC Player of the Year award in 1985. Mike Singletary swept the top defensive awards. He was named NFL Defensive Player of the Year, as well as NFC Defensive Player of the Year. Ditka was named Coach of the Year by the Associated Press, United Press International, and the *Sporting News*.

There was no question that winning the Super Bowl really galvanized the city of Chicago, one of the best sports cities in America, if not the greatest. The White Sox won the World Series in 2005. And the Bulls enjoyed amazing success in the 1990s, winning six NBA titles behind Michael Jordan. The Blackhawks got the city excited in 2010 with a Stanley Cup championship.

But I believe Chicago is foremost a Bears town and that the Super Bowl XX championship, regardless of how long ago that has been, ranks at the top of the list of titles won by a professional team in the Windy City. At least in modern times.

That is not to say that I do not give my props to the Blackhawks and White Sox, Bulls, and The Cubs. Winning a championship in any sport is an amazingly difficult feat. When the Bulls won all those titles, I believe people were more fans of Michael Jordan as an individual than the Bulls as a team.

Chicagoans seemed to be more excited about the Blackhawks winning their first Stanley Cup since 1961 than they did about the White Sox winning their first World Series since 1918. There just seems to be more baseball fans in Chicago who support the Cubs than the White Sox.

People had a swagger when they talked about our Bears championship because they know we would go out and kick ass and take names and come home with a victory. There was no doubt, there was no worry. It was all about taking care of business.

I remember taking a flight a couple of years ago and sitting next to a woman in her late 60s from Australia who had no idea who I was. She was talking about how the (current) Bears were not like the 1985 Bears and how much she loved Jim McMahon. She didn't know she was talking to me, and I just kept it like that. But the point of it is that through her accent and how she expressed herself, to me it was just amazing. She had me giggling inside. It was a poignant moment.

When I first came to Chicago, I came with the background that the team came first, not the individual. But when I got to Chicago, I found that the Bears had a lot of players with individual agendas. Everyone wanted to be recognized. Everyone wanted to be "The Man". When I first joined the team I felt like I was the kid from the small black school that no one really respected. They didn't know what I could do.

I felt more accepted by some of the other rookie players that I came in with in 1983, but not by anyone who was already on the team. I guess that is fairly common. I remember seeing established veteran defensive linemen like Dan Hampton, Steve McMichael, and Mike Hartenstine with their little clique. And some of the linebackers had their little exclusive group. The defensive backs didn't seem to stick together exclusively, but the offensive line had a lot of camaraderie.

Even though Walter Payton was a running back, I still paid a lot of attention to him, knowing that he *was* Chicago. Ditka often says how much he regrets not calling a play to give Payton a chance to score from close to the end zone in Super Bowl XX.

Walter never spoke publicly of any resentment about that missed opportunity, but I am sure it bothered him. And he said years later that it did bother him.

McMahon had scored on a 1-yard TD plunge in the third period of Super Bowl XX.

Ditka said he was too caught up in the euphoria of the game to immediately notice that Payton had not scored a TD.

"I really didn't realize it. I never thought about the individual thing so much," Ditka later said. "That was stupid on my part. That was probably the most disturbing thing in my career. That killed me. If I had one thing to do over again, I would make sure Payton took the ball into the end zone. I loved him; I had great respect for him. The only thing that really ever hurt me was when he didn't score in the Super Bowl."

As sad as it was that Payton did not score in the Super Bowl, a different set of circumstances conspired to prevent two of my friends – Al Harris and Todd Bell - from being a part of that Super Bowl team.

Harris sat out the entire 1985 season and Super Bowl XX because of a contract dispute. Represented by agent Ethan Locke, Harris sat out that season along with safety Todd Bell, who passed away March 16, 2005, at the age of 47. Harris returned to the Bears in 1986, but he said it took him until 1988 to get over the holdout because he felt disconnected from the rest of the organization. There was a period of time when he felt sorry for himself.

Harris says he is at peace now with the controversial business stance that unfortunately has defined his otherwise stellar playing career with the Bears.

He decided to remain in Chicago after his playing days to face the constant questions about his controversial decision. He says he feels blessed to have a wonderful family and friends and to have had an outstanding NFL career.

Harris played 11 seasons in the league with the Bears and Eagles, and he has a healthy perspective on life. He was taken aback in 2007 when he saw that linebacker Lance Briggs initially turned down a contract offer from the Bears for $7.2 million after he had made $700,000 the year before.

"I would have done cartwheels and backflips if the Bears had offered me 10 times what I had made in 1984," said Harris, who also played defensive end during his career.

Harris performed well for the Bears in 1984, but the team had drafted Wilber Marshall out of Florida, paying him nearly $500,000 a year.

In retrospect, Harris now realizes the Bears were in an awkward position with the desire to get Marshall on the field in 1985.

If free agency had been in place back then, Harris could have signed with another team. But that's how things worked then.

As great as our team was during the 1985 regular season and then in the playoffs, it's a shame that we were unable to win multiple Super Bowls. The Bears did not re-sign Willie Gault, and he went on to play with the Raiders. Wilber Marshall left to play with the Redskins, where he won another Super Bowl ring. McMahon suffered numerous injuries. Payton retired after the 1987 season, and Buddy Ryan left to become the head coach of the Philadelphia Eagles.

We were a team blessed with all sorts of incredible talent, but unless you can pull that talent together and have everybody focused in the same direction, you cannot win championships on a regular basis. Even though our defense continued to shine under new defensive coordinator Vince Tobin in 1986, we couldn t repeat to win the biggest game. Football remains the ultimate team sport, and everything has to go right to win it all. A little good luck doesn't hurt, either.

To show how naive I was at the time, I remember meeting future Hall of Famer Mike Singletary right after I got drafted. Mike was on the phone in the hallway at Halas Hall. I said to Mike, "What are you, a fullback, or running back, or what?" He looked at me real crazy. When he said he was a linebacker, I said, "You're a linebacker? A little dude like you? You're a linebacker?" That was our first exchange because we were all just there working out, not yet in positional groups.

Then I came across big Keith Van Horne, a 6-7, 285-pound offensive tackle. I said, "Man, you're huge!"

Van Horne was a talented player who was a mainstay on our offensive line that stuck together as a unit for about seven years. Van Horne played right tackle and Jim Covert was probably the best left tackle in Chicago Bears franchise history. The guards were Mark Bortz and Tom Thayer, and Jay Hilgenberg was the standout center. These guys helped pave the way for Payton to be such a productive ground gainer and for McMahon to be a very capable passer.

Gradually, I got to know a few other guys who kind of took me under their wing. Guys like Todd Bell, Jim Osborne, and Otis Wilson. I remember how outspoken Otis was and how he was able to back up his talk. Bruce Herron and Gary Campbell were other linebackers on the Bears when I first started. One of the first things to shock me about the professional game was watching some of my Bears teammates smoking in the locker room during halftime. Could anyone imagine that in today's society? I've seen old videos of coaches sneaking a smoke on the sideline during games. That seemed to be the only way for some of our veteran players to relax during those days.

A Week-by-Week Breakdown of Our Super Bowl Season

● ● ● ● ● ● ● ● ● ● ●

Week 1 Tampa Bay Buccaneers
Chicago 38, Tampa Bay 28
Bears 1-0

We were trailing 28-17 at the half to Tampa Bay. When we went into the locker room, I can remember everyone talking about the feeling we had when we lost to San Francisco in the NFC Championship game the year before and how we were going to dedicate ourselves to making amends for that. We kept referencing that conversation we had on the plane coming back to Chicago.

William "Refrigerator" Perry was strong, agile and extremely athletic. When Fridge clogged up the middle, I was able to take care of the outside. We worked very well in tandem to try to give opposing offenses fits. He was a rookie in 1985 and took the nation by storm with his extraordinary ability. (Photo courtesy of Mike Kinyon)

We were losing to one of the worst teams in the league, and we needed to take charge in the second half. Sure enough, right near the start of the second half, their quarterback, Steve DeBerg, throws a pass and I tip it. Leslie Frazier picks it off and takes it in for a touchdown from 29 yards out. We seized the momentum at that point and never looked back. Matt Suhey and Jim McMahon added touchdowns later. I was credited with two sacks and a tipped pass on the Frazier interception and touchdown.

Even though I am extremely proud of the individual statistics I was able to accrue – including sacks and fumble recoveries and such – the most important thing for us as a defensive unit was to win the game and do our part to insure a victory. The rest of it was gravy. A lot of times I was double-teamed, as were Hampton, Perry or McMichael. That would open up the floodgates for someone else to make a big play.

A lot of younger fans only know Leslie Frazier as the head coach of the Minnesota Vikings. But he was a terrific cornerback whose career was cut short by a knee injury sustained in Super Bowl XX. He was an intelligent player who was always around the football.

And Perry and McMichael don't receive enough credit for all they did over the years. When a defensive line is consistently able to clog up the middle, it enables the linebackers, safeties and cornerbacks to make more plays behind them. Fridge was strong, agile and tough, and he loved taking on the offensive linemen of the Bucs and showing them how athletic he was.

McMichael possessed the same qualities as Fridge, except he wasn't as heavy. Mongo loved to roll up his sleeves to show off his guns, even on a freezing cold day. McMichael was quick enough to slip in the gaps on the line and disrupt a play before it had a chance to develop. If he didn't get to the quarterback, he would trap a running back in the backfield or do something else to disrupt the rhythm of the play. Sometimes there is no statistic for that, but believe me, it was very important in terms of accomplishing what we wanted to do as a defense.

Tampa Bay was one of those teams that we generally dominated throughout the mid- to late 80s. But they were no pushover, and we knew we couldn't take plays off and still beat them.

• • • • • • • • • • •

Week 2 New England Patriots
Chicago 20, New England 7
Bears 2-0

Mike Singletary was a terrific student of the game who was able to extract every ounce of his ability to become a Hall of Fame linebacker. When we played the New England Patriots during the regular season in 1985, Singletary was credited with three sacks as we won 20-7. (Photo courtesy of Mike Kinyon)

The key to our victory over the Patriots was the fact we had very little respect for their running game. Craig James was their tailback and we bottled him up pretty well. I had fun in that game because I was able to play against my old friend and former teammate from Tennessee State, Steve Moore.

The Patriots were not the dominant team they are today, but we didn't want them to ever feel confident that they could match up and compete with us in '85. We almost made that mistake with Tampa Bay the week before. We had six sacks in the victory over New England. I had one, and Singletary was credited with three sacks. The Patriots were double-teaming me, so Singletary was able to blitz right up the middle from his linebacker position.

Buddy Ryan believed in constantly putting pressure on the quarterback to force him to make a decision quickly. He did not want the quarterback to feel comfortable in the backfield, and that was our responsibility as defensive players – to stay in the quarterback's face.

Payton was held to just 39 yards in that game because New England also had a strong defense. So it was up to our unit to provide great field position and create turnovers. We knew they couldn t run the ball against us, either.

One other remarkable aspect of Payton's game that some people often forget is that he was a terrific blocker. Even in a game like this one that saw the Patriots concentrate on slowing him down, Payton made himself a positive factor. As a receiver and as an occasional decoy, Payton was a player that the other teams always had to account for and keep an eye on. That created opportunities for other players to step up.

Of course, we didn't know at the time that we would meet up with New England again in the Super Bowl at the end of that season. It certainly did not hurt us to have had a regular-season game against them to get a feel for their strengths and weaknesses. Even in Super Bowl XX, the Patriots concentrated their efforts on slowing down Payton and our rushing game. But we obviously found other ways to score with our passing game and our dominant defense.

● ● ● ● ● ● ● ● ● ● ●

Week 3 at Minnesota Vikings
Chicago 33, Minnesota 24
Bears 3-0

This was a miraculous performance by Jim McMahon, who threw three touchdown passes in the second half. Steve Fuller started that Thursday night game in Minneapolis. When Fuller got hurt, McMahon begged to come in and play. McMahon busted the game open by hitting deep touchdown passes to Willie Gault and Dennis McKinnon.

Jim McMahon, shown here surveying the field for a possible deep pass, had an incredible knack for coming up with big plays when we needed them the most. His career stats may not be of Hall of Fame quality, but his gutsy performances were to be admired. (Photo courtesy of Mike Kinyon)

The one thing about McMahon that I really admired was his ability to disregard whatever criticism or abuse he was getting from the coaches. Once he got out there on the field and up under center, he took control of that offense and did his job. That attitude holds true no matter what you do in

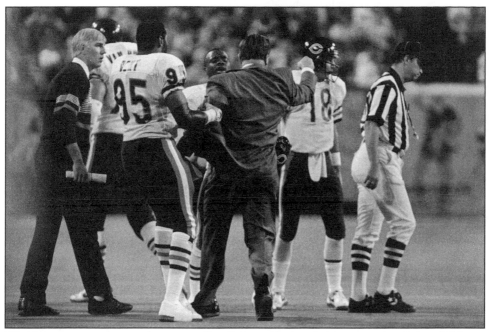

Mike Ditka was an equal-opportunity screamer. He yelled at rookies, he yelled at veterans, he yelled at officials. We often had to hold him back during the games. He reserved some of his most famous rants for his quarterbacks. (Photo Courtesy of AP Images)

life. If you don't take control of situations, you are bound to be controlled by somebody else.

I shared a sack with Ron Rivera in that win over the Vikings, and Steve McMichael had two sacks. Dan Hampton also had a sack. We set a team record that year for sacks. We also forced three interceptions in that game by Leslie Frazier, Wilber Marshall, and Otis Wilson.

We put constant pressure on the Vikings' quarterback because it was impossible to double-team all of us. We had a good way of supporting one another. That's how that season went.

There seemed to be something special about playing a nationally-televised game, whether it was on Monday night, Thursday night or whenever. So McMahon s heroics on this Thursday night contest really caught the attention of fans and media across the country who may not have realized just how good a team we had.

McMahon may not have had Hall of Fame statistics as a quarterback during his career, but he certainly had a knack for making big plays in big moments. This game was a perfect example of that. Sometimes we all get too caught up in the numbers and fail to ask just how many games did a player help his team win.

Jimmy Mac was his own man and he was not shy about standing up for what he believed in, whether he was talking to teammates, coaches or management.

● ● ● ● ● ● ● ● ● ● ●

Week 4 Washington Redskins
Chicago 45, Washington 10
Bears 4-0

The Redskins jumped out to a 10-0 lead before we scored 31 points in the second period and went on to a 45-10 rout. No deficit seemed insurmountable to us at this point. We felt pretty much invincible as we gained even more confidence with each victory.

I remember yapping at Redskins coach Joe Gibbs throughout this game because he acted as if he had something against me or something. The Redskins had George Rogers and John Riggins running the football for them. They kept trying to run their signature counter trey play against us to try to take advantage of our safety, Gary Fencik. Finally, Rogers ran another counter trey play, and Fencik whacked him pretty good. There was blood all over the place, but the Redskins just kept chattering along the sideline.

That jabbering back and forth with opponents is an aspect of the game that I really miss. Fans don't get the opportunity to hear all of the give-and-take between players on the field which sort of spices up the intensity of the game. As a defensive player, that kind of chatter used to get my juices flowing and helped me concentrate on the task at hand. You would forget about how

We had a pretty animated rivalry going with the Washington Redskins during the 1980s, especially. The Redskins were proud of their big offensive linemen and the way they protected their quarterback. But I took that as a challenge to beat them with my quickness and toss their quarterback to the ground. In this case, Joe Theismann is my victim. (Photo Courtesy of AP Images)

tired you were getting in the fourth quarter of a game when your mind was set on quieting a yapping opponent lining up in front of you.

I was able to record another sack, going against the Redskins big tackle, Joe Jacoby. I remember getting some hits and hurries on their quarterback, Joe Theismann, as well.

When you watch film of an upcoming opponent such as the Redskins that year, you check out a lot of little things that might help you do your job better during the game. For example, we would look for certain keys in their alignment that might tip off a certain play they like to run. Did an offensive lineman lean one way or the other in his stance to try to get a quicker start in the direction of the play called? I would look at how many drop steps a quarterback like Theismann would like to take. I would try to look at a quarterback's eyes to see if he had a tendency to signal where he was planning to throw the ball.

This was my third year in the league, so these so-called little things were becoming more and more important to my development. Mastering these little things made me a better player.

• • • • • • • • • • •

Week 5 at Tampa Bay Buccaneers
Chicago 27, Tampa Bay 19
Bears 5-0

Here came those pesky Tampa Bay Bucs again, and we beat them for the second time in just over a month. Tampa Bay always had some outstanding individual players who were able to keep their team within striking distance for at least part of the game.

I remember Walter Payton making a hell of a run against the great Tampa Bay linebacker, Hugh Green, from 9 yards out for a touchdown. To me, just watching Walter do his thing motivated me to play at that level at all times. For once, we did not record any sacks as a team because Steve DeBerg had a pretty quick release. But I did get some hits on him as soon as he released the ball. It was a warm day down in Tampa and they always seemed to play us tough.

Even during games where you don't get to the quarterback for a sack, it is possible to rattle them with hurries and batted passes at the line of scrimmage. And if you are able to get a lick in on the quarterback just as he releases a pass, you can still affect the trajectory and accuracy of a pass to

We generally played pretty well against Tampa Bay, but the Bucs often put up a good fight, especially on their home field. We prevailed in Week 5 of our Super Bowl championship season to improve to 5-0, but it wasn't an easy victory. (Photo Courtesy of AP Images)

force an interception or incompletion. The other thing we were able to do as defensive linemen and linebackers in that game was destroy the rhythm of the passing game. We made DeBerg get rid of the ball quicker than he wanted on occasion.

It was always a challenge for us to deal with the excessive heat in Tampa, especially early in the season. I probably lost a few pounds as the weight melted off me. But I preferred playing in those conditions much more than the frigid cold in places like Green Bay and Chicago in November and December.

• • • • • • • • • • •

Week 6 at San Francisco 49ers
Chicago 26, San Francisco 10
Bears 6-0

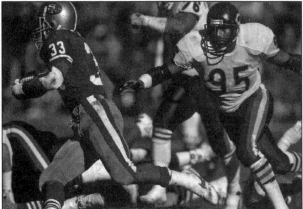

This was another one of those statement games for us. After losing to the 49ers in the NFC Championship game in '84, it was time for some payback. We won this one as Payton had a great rushing game and William Perry was unveiled in the backfield. I had two sacks and Wilber Marshall

Roger Craig was a versatile running back for San Francisco, but we were able to hold him in check in 1985 when we beat the 49ers 26-10 at Candlestick Park. Here I am zeroing in on Craig, who wound up gaining 42 yards on the day and one reception. It was sweet revenge to beat the 49ers after they had destroyed our dream in the previous year's playoffs. (Photo courtesy of Mike Kinyon)

had a pair of sacks from his linebacker position. We were really clicking then. At that point, we had renegotiated my contract. The Bears did not want to talk about adding to my base salary. They wanted to talk about incentives. So the Bears provided numerous incentives in my contract and made them applicable immediately. Now I had a chance to make some more money and I was quite happy about that. With all of the incentives, it was possible to put me up in the $1 million range. So we all were in a very good mood after that victory. We had bought a lot of wine in San Francisco, and we celebrated on the plane ride home.

After the plane landed at O'Hare Airport, we went our separate ways. I remember seeing on the I-294 toll road Coach Ditka's car sitting off to the side. The next day we all learned that he was stopped for a DWI. Usually, Ditka's wife, Dianna, would pick him up at the airport, but this time she had gone on the trip to San Francisco and stayed out there.

We all were extremely happy about the victory in San Francisco, but the media attention surrounding Coach Ditka's situation sort of detracted from what happened on the playing field.

• • • • • • • • • •

Week 7 Green Bay Packers
Chicago 23, Green Bay 7
Bears 7-0

As we approached the midway point of the season, things were starting to get serious, and fans everywhere were taking notice of our auspicious start. We improved to 7-0 after our convincing 23-7 victory over the Packers on a Monday Night Football telecast.

We improved our record to 7-0 after a 23-7 win against Green Bay in 1985. Steve McMichael (shown here) was credited with 1.5 sacks as our defense combined for five sacks against quarterbacks Lynn Dickey, Randy Wright and Jim Zorn. (Photo courtesy of Mike Kinyon)

Green Bay had scored first on a 27-yard touchdown pass from Lynn Dickey to James Lofton, but we shut them down after that. William Refrigerator Perry made his Monday Night Football debut in the backfield, scoring a touchdown. I had a sack and Dan Hampton had 1.5 sacks; McMichael had 1.5 and Otis Wilson had one.

I know I had a lot of hits that night, and it was the unveiling of the Fridge, so America really got its money's worth in terms of entertainment and novelty performances.

We were all happy for Fridge. He was very athletic for his size. I always felt I could have done something similar offensively. I played fullback when I was younger, and I knew I could play tight end. I knew I could sustain a block, and I knew I could catch a ball. That is what I used to do. Even when I was a defensive end in the pros, during warm-ups, the first thing I would do was go over by the receivers to catch the ball, because to me, it was all about concentration. Visual concentration. And sometimes I would line up with the defensive backs during practice to work on my cardio endurance. Good quickness, footwork and agility can come in handy at any position. It was something I just enjoyed doing.

I remember on the day after that game against the Packers, a young lady I had dated in college showed up unannounced in Chicago. I remember later getting calls from my mother and the young lady's mother. I was at practice, and there she was sitting at the front door with her luggage and everything. I am trying to go out the back door of our training facility and Buddy Ryan and all of the other players are yelling to the girl: "There he is! There he is – over there!"

So I had to get after the guys for doing that. I think the Bears helped her out later by putting her up in a hotel while she hung around for a couple of days. I felt bad about the situation, but how can you show up like that? I knew she was going through something emotionally, but I had not seen her for three or four years since college. It was an awkward situation, and it was a little scary.

There are times when your personal life and your past sometimes interfere with what you are trying to accomplish career-wise. This was one of those occasions.

● ● ● ● ● ● ● ● ● ● ●

Week 8 Minnesota Vikings
Chicago 27, Minnesota 9
Bears 8-0

We dominated the Vikings from the start of this game, collecting 24 first downs to their 16. We also doubled their total yardage while creating five Viking turnovers. Minnesota's quarterback then was Tommy Kramer, and he was a tough guy who took a lot of beatings from us. I remember hitting him a lot, but he would stand tall in the pocket. They kept trying to hit us with the slant pass over the middle. Their running backs were Leo Lewis and Darren Nelson, and Steve Jordan was a very good tight end.

• • • • • • • • • • •

Week 9 at Green Bay Packers
Chicago 16, Green Bay 10
Bears 9-0

We ran our record to 9-0 with a tough 16-10 win over our rival Packers at Lambeau Field. We scored nine points in the fourth quarter to gain the victory. That was the first game that we hit Fridge Perry with a pass play. He caught a 4-yard touchdown pass from McMahon. Steve McMichael was credited with a safety in the fourth quarter to make it 10-9. Then Payton ran for a touchdown for the game-winner.

Those games were always grudge matches, and you really had to earn a victory, no matter the record of each team.

I believe it was after this Green Bay game that we started working on the Super Bowl Shuffle. That's when the information first came to us about it. We went over to Richard Meyers' house to shoot the lyrics to the song; he had a studio in his house. By the following week, the record was out on the streets and people were playing it.

• • • • • • • • • • •

Week 10 Detroit Lions
Chicago 24, Detroit 3
Bears 10-0

Steve Fuller really helped us get going in this game at Soldier Field that improved our record to 10-0. We realized what kind of team we had and what sort of opportunity was ahead of us. Lions running back Billy Simms used to remind me of a Walter Payton-type player. He wasn't as strong as Walter, but he was very shifty and difficult to bring down. Simms wasn't as powerful as Walter, yet he was powerful enough to run you over on occasion. He had great quickness and head, shoulder and hips movement. And he ran with a violent abandon. To me, he had the leg strength of Walter; he just didn't have the upper-body strength of Walter. But he was someone you had to deal with when you came to play the Lions. When you start talking about Hall of Fame players, you are talking about someone you have to account for in order to win the game. That was Billy Simms.

● ● ● ● ● ● ● ● ● ● ●

Week 11 at Dallas Cowboys
Chicago 44, Dallas 0
Bears 11-0

Blanking the Cowboys 44-0 in Dallas was one of the sweetest victories in Bears history. I opened that game with an interception and easy touchdown after Dan Hampton hit the ball. I also had two sacks. It was an important victory for Coach Ditka because he was playing against his old mentor, Tom Landry. He wanted to win so badly, even though he tried to play it down leading up to that game. The Cowboys were considered America's Team, and we wanted to kick America's Team's ass. We wanted to be that team everyone loved. And we were the youngest team in the league at that time. I remember seeing Gil Brandt of the Cowboys' front office on the sideline with his big hat before the game. The Cowboys had disappointed me before the draft in 1983.

I didn't do my workouts for them before the draft. Back in those days, if you had a good workout for the Cowboys, they would say great things about you and you could go up the draft charts. Since I didn't work out for them, I moved down the charts. So I told Gil Brandt, "You know, I owe you an ass-whupping today." And he looked at me crazy.

On artificial turf, I knew that I could be a step quicker. On grass, I knew that I could be more shifty, because grass gives. On turf, the game becomes a little bit quicker.

We managed to hold Hall of Fame running back Tony Dorsett to 44 yards on 12 carries in that game. I remember meeting Dorsett and Ed Too Tall Jones in Nashville, Tennessee, when I was still in college. It was a big thrill, and now I was getting a chance to play against them. There wasn't a greater moment. And the game was in Dallas, my first time there.

• • • • • • • • • •

Week 12 Atlanta Falcons
Chicago 36, Atlanta 0
Bears 12-0

We continued our undefeated ways against the Atlanta Falcons at Soldier Field in Week 12, blanking them 36-0. That was pretty much a beating there, and we dominated the Falcons in every way possible. That was typical of the way we went about our business with all opponents that season. The Falcons fell to 2-10, and that was another example of us taking care of business by imposing our will against a weaker ballclub. You can't let a team that is down like the Falcons were then, play with you. Gerald Riggs and Joe Washington were their running backs then, and David Archer was the Atlanta quarterback. I had 1.5 sacks against Archer. Henry Waechter had 2.5 sacks and "The Fridge" had another sack. Offensively, Walter Payton rushed for 102 yards on a 20-degree day in Chicago.

• • • • • • • • • •

Week 13 at Miami Dolphins
Miami 38, Chicago 24
Bears 12-1

Week 13 proved to be unlucky for us in our bid to go undefeated. The Dolphins prevailed 38-24, exploiting our weaknesses, and we did not play to our strength, which is running the football. We got lured into a passing game and the Dolphins did a better job with Dan Marino at quarterback, even though I was able to get two sacks against him. It was a Monday Night Football game and the players wanted to go down to Miami a littler earlier in the week to become accustomed to the change in weather conditions during practices. As players, we had looked at the schedule and figured if we could get past the Dolphins, we would have an excellent chance to go unbeaten the rest of the way. Dan Hampton and some of the other players talked to Ditka about going down early to get ready for the Dolphins. But Ditka wouldn't do it because Buddy Ryan had presented the idea to him. Now, if Ditka had come up with the idea himself, it probably would have been cool. So when we got down there, our starting quarterback McMahon wasn't available, and the Dolphins had been last in the league as far as stopping the run. But we went down there trying to do what they did – throw the football. It made no sense, especially with our backup quarterback.

Toward the end of the game, McMahon went in and made sure Payton kept his consecutive 100-yard game streak intact, even though Ditka was calling for McMahon to throw the ball.

● ● ● ● ● ● ● ● ● ●

Week 14 Indianapolis Colts
Chicago 17, Indianapolis 10
Bears 13-1

We rebounded after that tough loss in Miami to beat the Colts, 17-10, at Soldier Field. It didn't seem as if that game should have been as close as the final score indicated, because we dominated the stats, including total yards and time of possession. But we survived and improved our record to 13-1.

It seems remarkable that the Colts franchise would become so strong in later years when Jim Harbaugh and Peyton Manning led them. That shows you the importance of having a premier quarterback and what he can mean to your franchise. Very rarely do you find teams that are so well-balanced as we were in 1985. We had a dominating defense, a great running game led by Walter Payton, a gutsy, clutch quarterback in McMahon, and one of the best kickers in the league in Kevin Butler, who was just a rookie in '85.

• • • • • • • • • • •

Week 15 at New York Jets
Chicago 19, New York 6
Bears 14-1

Next up was a trip to the Big Apple to face the Jets. I remember having a good game against the Jets, collecting a pair of sacks. And I almost had an interception. It was a lot of fun that day. We held the Jets to just 70 yards rushing and only 89 yards through the air. It was another dominating defensive performance. We never let up.

• • • • • • • • • • •

Week 16 at Detroit Lions
Chicago 37, Detroit 17
Bears 15-1

The final regular-season game of the 1985 season was against the Lions in the Silverdome, and we romped 37-17 after leading only 6-3 at the half. I finished off the regular season with two more sacks. We had six sacks among us. Tyrone Keys, Wilber Marshall, and William Perry joined in the fun against quarterback Erik Hipple. I remember getting in the backfield and holding Hipple in my arms while Wilber Marshall hit him so hard that I ended up stepping right in Hipple's face at the end of the play when he hit the ground. I don't know how it happened, but Marshall just knocked Hipple out of my hands. I remember seeing Hipple sprawled out on the ground knocked out, with his hands over his head. I started signaling to the Lions' bench to get this man some help. That was a brutal game for a quarterback that I really felt sorry for. We weren't giving him any mercy and the Lions weren't giving him any blocking help. We were just blowing past their blockers and knocking the hell out of Hipple. You would think they would try to get rid of the ball quicker or run some draw plays to keep us off balance.

Playoffs

* * * * * * * * * * *

NFC Divisional Playoff – New York Giants
Chicago 21, New York 0

We dominated the game defensively by allowing only 32 yards rushing and sacking Giants quarterback Phil Simms for 60 yards. Our first touchdown came on a New York punt attempt from their own 12-yard line. Sean Landeta whiffed on it and

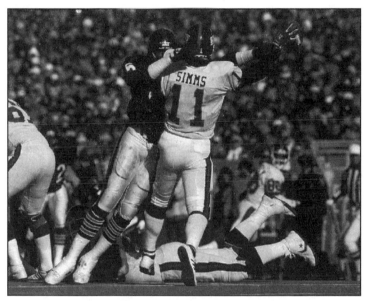

We rolled over the New York Giants 21-0 in the NFC divisional playoff game at Soldier Field following the 1985 regular season. Here I am dumping Giants quarterback Phil Simms, who lost 60 yards on sacks during that game. (Photo courtesy of Mike Kinyon)

Shaun Gayle picked up the ball and ran 5 yards for an easy touchdown.

When it's your year to win a championship, it's as if everything goes your way. When Landeta whiffed on the punt, it seemed as if an especially stiff breeze shifted the ball out of his hands and forced him to miss the football. I don't think I have ever seen anything so strange in my life. But that was just the kind of year we had in '85.

● ● ● ● ● ● ● ● ● ● ●

NFC Championship – Los Angeles Rams
Chicago 24, Los Angeles 0

We limited Rams running back Eric Dickerson to 46 yards and held
quarterback Dieter Brock to 10 out of 31 attempts for 66 passing yards.
The Rams only gained 130 yards of total offense. Jim McMahon scored on a
16-yard touchdown run in the first quarter and threw a 22-yard touchdown
pass to Willie Gault in the third quarter. Kicker Kevin Butler kicked a 34-yard
field goal in the first period. In the fourth quarter, I forced Brock to fumble
and Wilber Marshall picked up the loose ball and returned it 52 yards for a
touchdown.

In yet another surreal scene at Soldier Field, the snow began to fall just at
the moment that Marshall picked up the fumble and began racing for the end
zone. Papa Bear Halas must have been smiling down on us that day.

We were able to hold Rams star running back Eric Dickerson to 46 yards rushing in the NFC Championship game
before Super Bowl XX. Here I am putting the finishing touches on Dickerson along with teammates Mike Singletary
and Gary Fencik. (Photo courtesy of Mike Kinyon)

• • • • • • • • • • •

Super Bowl at New England Patriots

Chicago 46, New England 10

Bears are World Champions

The New England Patriots tried a variety of tactics to try to slow me down, both during the regular season and in Super Bowl XX. In this photo, John Hannah tries to muscle me. I wound up winning the Super Bowl MVP trophy after recording 1.5 sacks, a blocked pass and two forced fumbles as we won 46-10. (Photo courtesy of Mike Kinyon)

We took care of business right after the Patriots grabbed a quick early lead following a turnover. Larry McGrew had recovered a fumble by Payton at our 19-yard line on the second play of the game, setting up Tony Franklin's 36-yard field goal. That was their highlight of the game. We came back with a 7-play, 59-yard drive, featuring a 43-yard pass completion from McMahon to Gault. We never looked back after that. The rout was on.

I proudly received the Super Bowl XX MVP award.

Unfinished Business 15

Relatively speaking, there haven't been that many years since I last suited up for an NFL game, yet I am able to view the league from a much clearer perspective as time has passed. I am still troubled by the politics of the game and the heartless business of professional football. I feel players continue to be exploited for the greater financial gain of those associated with the league off the field. Yes, players are compensated in record proportions, but what price can be placed on your health and well-being long-term in life?

Every day, it seems, I pick up the paper or turn on the television and see disturbing stories about current and former NFL players dying young, far too many taking their own lives. I cringed when I read about former Tennessee Titans wide receiver O.J. Murdock apparently taking his own life with a gunshot wound to the chest at the age of 25 on July 30, 2012.

Two weeks earlier came the sad news that former NFL defensive lineman Cleveland Elam had passed away at the age of 60. Elam was a fellow Tennessee State alum, and I looked up to him and followed his career in the NFL. As a member of the San Francisco 49ers, Elam collected 17.5 sacks in 1977, and he was a two-time Pro Bowl player who finished his career with the Detroit Lions. While Elam wasn't exactly a young man, I thought he looked great when I last saw him. I still have the picture on my cell phone of him and me together that was taken the night we had a roast for our former Tennessee State coach, Joe Gilliam.

Even when some former players live a so-called normal life span, quite often their quality of life is compromised because of what they were encouraged to do as players. I am talking about the easy access to pain-killers, shots and other mind-numbing drugs which had disastrous effects on the kidneys or other organs. We were encouraged to play through pain and injury to help our team win. But what about the welfare of the individual?

Most of us are out of the game of football before the age of 40 and hope to have many more decades of high-quality life ahead of us. But that so often is not the case, and it seems to me there is no great urgency by the league to take care of its former players. We are used, discarded, and replaced by younger, fresher legs. And then the cycle continues as long as young men are willing to sacrifice their bodies for the sake of big bucks.

Of course, football is not for everybody, especially at the highest level. There is inherent danger and risk of injury, and we assume that challenge as players. But we are more than pieces of meat, and it is beyond the point of the league accepting a greater responsibility for its players – both morally and legally.

It has long been my belief that the NFL should provide health insurance for its former players for their entire lives. Because of the documented list of long-term ailments associated with playing professional football, it is unbelievable to me that players are not cared for in the manner they should be when it comes to health insurance.

As young men, we all feel quite invincible, and we believe somehow that we can overcome any physical, mental or emotional obstacle. NOT TRUE! The truth is that more of us need to admit to our shortcomings and not be ashamed to ask for help when it is available. Whether those personal issues involve drugs, alcohol, domestic problems or legal issues, we have to be more self-aware and responsibile.

I have been blessed to have had a life filled with team championships and, ultimately, Pro Football Hall of Fame recognition. But I am no different than anybody else when it comes to dealing with personal issues that set us back and tug on our emotions.

Even in my moment of greatest personal achievement – when I was named the Most Valuable Player of Super Bowl XX with the Bears – I never will forget the moment when I stood by my locker holding the MVP trophy and not one person came over to talk to me. The champagne was not flowing. Everything seemed quiet. That had to be the most emotionally conflicted moment in my life.

If I can convey a lasting message about what I have learned in my life in football, it would be that the NFL needs to take greater responsibility for what is happening to its players. Millions and millions of dollars are flowing between the hands of team owners, but all is not so great with the players from a physical and emotional standpoint. Something is missing; something is horribly wrong with this picture.

A person without a conscience is a deadly person. The most important thing that God could ever give a person is a conscience. Everybody has it, but not everybody uses it. Your conscience allows you to do and understand right and wrong. If you have a conscience, you know there is something spiritual out there. Do the right thing.

APPENDIX

Richard Lamar Dent

Position: DE

Height: 6-5 Weight: 265 lbs.

Born: December 13, 1960 in Atlanta, GA

College: Tennessee St.

Drafted: Chicago Bears in the 8th round (203rd overall) of the 1983 NFL Draft.

Awards: 4-time Pro Bowler & 1-time First-Team All-Pro

Inducted into Hall of Fame in 2011: Finalist in 2004, 2005, 2007, 2008, 2009, 2010

							DEF INTERCEPTIONS					FUMBLES					TACKLES			
YEAR	AGE	TM	POS	G	GS	SK	INT	YDS	TD	LNG	PD	FF	FMB	FR	YDS	TD	TKL	AST	SFTY	AV
1983	23	CHI	DE	16	3	3.0						1	0	0	0	0	12	0		3
1984*	24	CHI	RDE	16	10	17.5						4	0	1	0	0	39	0		14
1985*+	25	CHI	RDE	16	16	17.0	2	10	1	9	0	7	0	2	0	0	38	0		19
1986	26	CHI	RDE	15	14	11.5						4	0	0	0	0	75	0		9
1987	27	CHI	RDE	12	12	12.5						4	0	2	11	0	34	0		7
1988	28	CHI	RDE	13	12	10.5						3	0	1	0	0	61	0		14
1989	29	CHI	RDE	15	15	9.0	1	30	0	30	0	2	0	2	0	0	70	0		7
1990*	30	CHI	RDE	16	16	12.0	3	21	0	15	0	2	0	3	45	1	81	0		16
1991	31	CHI	RDE	16	16	10.5	1	4	0	4	0	0	0	1	0	0	84	0		8
1992	32	CHI	RDE	16	16	8.5						6	0	1	0	0	82	0		7
1993*	33	CHI	RDE	16	16	12.5	1	24	0	24	0	1	0	0	0	0	64	0		12
1994	34	SFO	DE	2	2	2.0											7	1		1
1995	35	CHI	DE	3	1												1	0		1
1996	36	IND	DE	16	1	6.5						2	0	0	0	0	13	2	1	2
1997	37	PHI		15	0	4.5						1	0	0	0	0	10	3		2
Career				203	150	137.5	8	89	1	30	0	37	0	13	56	1	671	6	1	122
12 yrs		CHI		170	147	124.5	8	89	1	30	0	34	0	13	56	1	641	0		117
1 yr		IND		16	1	6.5						2	0	0	0	0	13	2	1	2
1 yr		PHI		15	0	4.5						1	0	0	0	0	10	3		2
1 yr		SFO		2	2	2.0											7	1		1

*Selected to the Pro Bowl   +Named First Team All-Pro

About the Authors

Richard Dent made quite a name for himself in the National Football League after toiling in relative obscurity at tiny Tennessee State University. The Chicago Bears drafted the then tall and skinny Dent in the eighth round of the 1983 draft. He would grow to 6-5, 265 lbs., and go on to become the storied franchise's all-time leader in quarterback sacks.

In 1985, Dent led the NFL with 17 quarterback sacks and the Bears went on to wallop the New England Patriots 46-10 as he was named the Most Valuable Player in Super Bowl XX.

Dent later joined the San Francisco 49ers as a free agent in 1994, although he missed most of that season with an injury. He returned to the Bears in 1995 before joining the Indianapolis Colts the next season. Dent retired after spending the 1997 season with the Philadelphia Eagles. Dent was inducted into the Pro Football Hall of Fame in 2011.

Since retiring from pro football, Dent has been very active in the Chicago community.

Since joining the *Chicago Tribune* in 1974, Fred Mitchell has covered the Cubs, Bulls and Bears beats, and now also writes a weekly column. He appears regularly on Chicago television. Mitchell, who has been involved in numerous civic activities, lives in Chicago with his wife, Kim, and son, Cameron.

www.ascendbooks.com

*Visit www.ascendbooks.com for more great titles
on your favorite teams and athletes.*